Better Homes and Gardens®

SALADS

BETTER HOMES AND GARDENS® BOOKS

Editor Gerald M. Knox
Art Director Ernest Shelton
Managing Editor David A. Kirchner
Copy and Production Editors James D. Blume, Marsha Jahns, Rosanne Weber Mattson, Mary Helen Schiltz

Food and Nutrition Editor Nancy Byal
Department Head, Cook Books Sharyl Heiken
Associate Department Heads Sandra Granseth, Rosemary C. Hutchinson, Elizabeth Woolever
Senior Food Editors Julia Malloy, Marcia Stanley, Joyce Trollope
Associate Food Editors Barbara Atkins, Linda Henry, Mary Jo Plutt, Maureen Powers, Martha Schiel, Linda Foley Woodrum
Recipe Development Editor Marion Viall
Test Kitchen Director Sharon Stilwell
Test Kitchen Photo Studio Director Janet Pittman
Test Kitchen Home Economists Jean Brekke, Kay Cargill, Marilyn Cornelius, Jennifer Darling, Maryellyn Krantz, Lynelle Munn, Dianna Nolin, Marge Steenson, Cynthia Volcko

Associate Art Directors Linda Ford Vermie, Neoma Alt West, Randall Yontz
Assistant Art Directors Lynda Haupert, Harijs Priekulis, Tom Wegner
Senior Graphic Designers Jack Murphy, Stan Sams, Darla Whipple-Frain
Graphic Designers Mike Burns, Sally Cooper, Blake Welch, Brian Wignall, Kimberly Zarley

Vice President, Editorial Director Doris Eby
Executive Director, Editorial Services Duane L. Gregg

President, Book Group Fred Stines
Director of Publishing Robert B. Nelson
Vice President, Retail Marketing Jamie Martin
Vice President, Direct Marketing Arthur Heydendael

Salads
Editor Maureen Powers
Copy and Production Editor Rosanne Weber Mattson
Graphic Designer Lynda Haupert
Electronic Text Processor Donna Russell
Photographers Michael Jensen and Sean Fitzgerald
Food Stylists Suzanne Finley, Dianna Nolin, Janet Pittman, Maria Rolandelli

On the cover
Seafood Salad (see recipe, page 97)

Our seal assures you every recipe in *Salads*
has been tested in the Better Homes and Gardens® Test Kitchen.
This means that each recipe is practical and reliable,
and meets our high standards of taste appeal.

Salads fit every occasion. Toss them or tote them. Make them elegant and sophisticated or quick and casual. Make them a main dish or simply make them ahead. Serve them before the dinner entrée, as a main course for lunch, or as a side dish with supper. Light and refreshing, salads make any mealtime memorable.

So, sample a bowl of fresh greens delicately wilted in a hot bacon dressing or try a simple three-bean salad with a delightful dill marinade. Or, create an extravagant, shimmering gelatin salad. No matter what your menu, you'll find lots of time-tested salads, as well as delicious new creations.

You decide what sounds best. Then, let *Salads* provide you with the know-how and the show-how to make *your* kind of salad.

Contents

Simple Tossed Salads

A wooden bowl filled with a variety of crisp greens topped with a rich salad dressing—it's enough to make your mouth water. Fresh salads like these are simple and always sensational.

Survey our selection of refreshing salads. You'll discover recipes that satisfy your discriminating palate, yet don't tax your time and energy.

Tomato-Parmesan Toss

This salad says simple sophistication when you top it off with your favorite purchased salad dressing or one of the delicious homemade dressings in this book.

Salad greens*
18 **cherry tomatoes, halved**
¼ **cup grated Parmesan cheese**
3 **slices bacon, crisp-cooked, drained, and crumbled,** *or* **3 tablespoons packaged bacon pieces**
½ **cup desired salad dressing**

Core iceberg lettuce; remove core (see photo 1). Rinse head under running water (see photo 2). Place, core end down, in colander to drain. If using other greens, rinse under running water. Remove stem from spinach. Remove center vein from romaine leaves (see photo 3). Pat greens dry (see photo 4).

Tear enough greens into bite-size pieces to measure 6 cups. Place any remaining greens in a plastic bag or crisper. Store in the refrigerator.

In a salad bowl place torn greens and cherry tomatoes. Sprinkle with Parmesan cheese and bacon. Pour dressing over salad. Toss to coat. Makes 6 servings.

---

*Choose from iceberg lettuce, Boston lettuce, Bibb lettuce, romaine, leaf lettuce, spinach, watercress, chicory, escarole, sorrel, or rocket (see pages 114–117).

1 After purchase, check the lettuce for any wilted or discolored outer leaves. Remove and discard them. Loosen the lettuce core by hitting the stem end of the head sharply on your kitchen countertop. Twist the core, then remove and discard it.

2 Place the head of lettuce, bottom side up, under cold running water. Rinse several times to clean the leaves. Drain the lettuce by inverting the head in a colander set in the sink or on a draining

3 Cut the bottom core from romaine, Boston, or Bibb lettuce. Separate the leaves and rinse. Remove center vein from romaine by cutting down both sides of the vein, as shown.

4 Place the rinsed greens on several layers of paper towels or on a clean kitchen towel. Place another paper towel over the greens. Pat gently to remove the water clinging to the leaves. Try to remove as much water as possible. Water that clings to the greens dilutes the flavor and consistency of the salad dressing and makes the salad soggy.

Chutney Salad

Chutney is a thick, sweet-tasting relish made from fruits or vegetables. Try apple or mango chutney for a fruity-tasting dressing.

 4 **cups torn romaine *or* salad greens (see pages 8–9)**
 ¼ **cup raisins**
 ¼ **cup peanuts**
 ¼ **cup plain yogurt**
 2 **tablespoons finely chopped chutney**
 1 **tablespoon milk**
 ¼ **teaspoon curry powder**

In a salad bowl place torn romaine or greens, raisins, and peanuts.

For dressing, in a small bowl stir together yogurt, chutney, milk, and curry powder. Pour dressing over salad. Toss to coat. Serves 4.

Crouton Salad Bowl

 4 **cups torn Boston lettuce *or* salad greens (see pages 8–9)**
 ½ **cup shredded Swiss cheese (2 ounces)**
 ½ **cup herb-seasoned croutons**
 ⅓ **cup bottled Caesar salad dressing**

In a salad bowl place torn lettuce or greens. Add cheese and croutons. Pour dressing over salad. Toss to coat. Makes 4 servings.

French-Onion Fling

To enjoy French-fried onions that are crunchy and crispy, serve this salad right after tossing it.

 4 **cups torn iceberg lettuce *or* salad greens (see pages 8–9)**
 1 **cup sliced fresh mushrooms**
 1 **3-ounce can French-fried onions**
 ⅓ **cup desired salad dressing**

In a salad bowl place torn lettuce or greens, mushrooms, and onions. Pour dressing over salad. Toss to coat. Makes 4 servings.

Beet-Spinach Salad

 6 **cups torn spinach *or* salad greens (see pages 8–9)**
 1 **8-ounce can sliced beets, drained**
 1 **small onion, sliced and separated into rings**
 ⅓ **cup bottled Italian salad dressing**
 ¼ **cup crumbled blue cheese *or* shredded cheddar cheese (1 ounce)**

In a large salad bowl combine torn spinach or greens, beets, and onion. Pour dressing over salad. Toss to coat. Sprinkle with blue or cheddar cheese. Makes 6 servings.

Greek-Style Salad

The flavor of an olive oil ranges from sweet and mellow to sharp and distinct. The type of olive and its origin determine the flavor of the olive oil.

8 cups torn spinach *or* salad greens
    (see pages 8–9)
½ cup crumbled feta cheese (2 ounces)
½ cup sliced pitted ripe olives
¼ cup broken walnuts
2 tablespoons lemon juice
2 tablespoons olive *or* salad oil
2 tablespoons honey
¼ teaspoon ground cinnamon

In a large salad bowl place torn spinach or greens, feta cheese, olives, and walnuts.

For dressing, in a screw-top jar combine lemon juice, oil, honey, and cinnamon. Cover and shake well. Pour dressing over salad. Toss to coat. Makes 8 servings.

Oriental Toss

Use the remaining water chestnuts for a stir fry. Just place leftover water chestnuts in a small container and cover with water. Cover and store in the refrigerator.

½ of a 6-ounce package frozen pea pods
4 cups torn salad greens
    (see pages 8–9)
½ of an 8-ounce can sliced water
    chestnuts, drained
1 tablespoon sesame seed
3 tablespoons salad oil
4 teaspoons vinegar
4 teaspoons dry sherry
2 teaspoons honey
2 teaspoons soy sauce

In a colander rinse pea pods under warm water to thaw. In a salad bowl place pea pods, torn greens, water chestnuts, and sesame seed.

For dressing, in a screw-top jar combine salad oil, vinegar, sherry, honey, and soy sauce. Cover and shake well. Pour dressing over salad. Toss to coat. Makes 6 servings.

Imaginative Iceberg!

There's a wide variety of salad greens available in supermarkets today, yet iceberg lettuce remains a popular choice. In your next salad, go beyond torn lettuce and try some different shapes.

Wedges: Cut the head lengthwise in half. Place each half, cut side down, on a cutting board. Cut each half lengthwise into thirds. Makes 6 wedges.

Shredded: Cut the head lengthwise in half. Place each half, cut side down, on a cutting board. Cut crosswise into long, coarse shreds. Makes about 4 cups.

Rafts: Cut the head crosswise into 1-inch-thick slices. Makes 4 to 6 rafts.

Chunks: Make rafts. Cut each raft crosswise and then lengthwise to get bite-size lettuce chunks. Makes about 4 cups.

Vegetable Salads

Crunch! Crispy, fresh vegetables make great-tasting salads. Follow along with us and we'll show you how to slice, dice, shred, and toss your way to home-style and company-special recipes.

Of course, the real fun comes when you sink your teeth into that delicious vegetable salad!

Vegetable Potpourri

Vegetable Potpourri

½ of a small head cabbage
¼ of a small head cauliflower
1 small zucchini
1 stalk celery
1 small carrot
¼ cup dairy sour cream
¼ cup bottled creamy cucumber
    salad dressing
1 teaspoon poppy seed
    Dash bottled hot pepper sauce

Cut cabbage into quarters. Shred cabbage (see photo 1). Cut cauliflower into small flowerets. Slice flowerets, if desired (see photo 2). Cut zucchini lengthwise in half, then cut into slices to form half-circles. Thinly bias-slice celery (see photo 3). Shred the carrot (see photo 4).

In a bowl combine cabbage, cauliflower, zucchini, celery, and carrot. For dressing, in a small bowl stir together sour cream, bottled salad dressing, poppy seed, and hot pepper sauce. Pour dressing over vegetable mixture. Toss to coat. Makes 6 servings.

2 Rinse the cauliflower under cold running water. Using a paring knife, remove green leaves and any brown spots. Cut or break cauliflower into flowerets. If desired, cut flowerets into thin slices, as shown.

3 Hold the celery stalk firmly against a cutting board. Holding a knife at an angle to the celery stalk, thinly slice the celery.

1 For coarse shreds, hold a quarter-head of cabbage firmly against the cutting board. Using a knife, slice the cabbage to make long, coarse shreds, as shown.

For medium shreds, push a quarter-head of cabbage across the coarse blade of a vegetable shredder. For fine shreds use your blender, following the manufacturer's directions.

4 Use a coarse shredder to shred the carrot. Hold the carrot at an angle to the shredding surface. Rub carrot along the surface from top to bottom. Use this technique for other vegetables when you want long, pretty shreds.

Julienne Carrots: Cut a peeled carrot crosswise in half. (You'll need to cut larger carrots into thirds.) Cut each carrot half or third lengthwise in half. Continue cutting each carrot stick lengthwise in half until they are thin, bite-size sticks.

You can also use this technique for cutting celery, cucumbers, zucchini, parsnips, turnips, meats, and cheeses.

Sweet 'n' Sour Salad

If you don't have a blender, quickly mix this dressing by hand. Just combine dressing ingredients in a small bowl and beat with a wire whisk.

1   **large cucumber, cut into julienne strips (see tip box, page 15)**
⅔   **cup coarsely shredded carrot (see photo 4, page 15)**
1   **tablespoon finely chopped green onion**
2   **tablespoons vinegar**
2   **tablespoons orange juice**
2   **tablespoons honey**
1   **tablespoon salad oil**
2   **tablespoons sunflower nuts**

In a bowl combine cucumber, carrot, and green onion. For dressing, in a blender container combine vinegar, orange juice, honey, and salad oil. Cover and blend for 30 seconds. Pour dressing over vegetable mixture. Toss to coat. Before serving, sprinkle sunflower nuts over salad. Makes 4 servings.

Crunchy Coleslaw

Top this colorful coleslaw with rich Creamy Dressing or toss it with tangy Vinaigrette Dressing—either choice tastes superb.

2½   **cups shredded cabbage (see photo 1, page 14)**
¾   **cup broccoli *or* cauliflower flowerets (see photo 2, page 14)**
⅓   **cup shredded carrot (see photo 4, page 15)**
⅓   **cup chopped green pepper**
2   **tablespoons thinly sliced green onion**
   Creamy Dressing *or* Vinaigrette Dressing

In a bowl combine cabbage, broccoli or cauliflower, carrot, green pepper, and onion. Pour Creamy or Vinaigrette Dressing over vegetable mixture. Toss to coat. Makes 6 servings.

Creamy Dressing: In a small bowl stir together ¼ cup *mayonnaise or salad dressing,* 2 teaspoons *sugar,* 2 teaspoons *vinegar,* ½ teaspoon *celery seed,* ¼ teaspoon *salt,* and ⅛ teaspoon *pepper.* Makes about ⅓ cup dressing.

Vinaigrette Dressing: In a screw-top jar combine 3 tablespoons *vinegar,* 2 tablespoons *salad oil,* 2 teaspoons *sugar,* ⅛ teaspoon *salt,* ⅛ teaspoon *garlic powder,* and 1 or 2 drops bottled *hot pepper sauce.* Cover and shake till combined. Makes about ⅓ cup dressing.

Broccoli-Mushroom Salad

2 cups broccoli flowerets (see photo 2, page 14)
1⅓ cups sliced fresh mushrooms
1 cup fresh bean sprouts
⅓ cup bottled Green Goddess salad dressing

In a bowl combine broccoli, mushrooms, and bean sprouts. Pour salad dressing over vegetable mixture. Toss to coat. Makes 4 servings.

Parsnip Salad

2 cups shredded parsnips (see photo 4, page 15)
½ cup sliced radishes
½ cup finely chopped green pepper
⅓ cup finely chopped celery
¼ cup plain yogurt
¼ cup bottled creamy Italian salad dressing
2 teaspoons sugar

In a bowl combine parsnips, radishes, green pepper, and celery. For dressing, in a small bowl stir together yogurt, bottled salad dressing, and sugar. Pour dressing over vegetable mixture. Toss to coat. Makes 4 servings.

The Chopping Block

It's puzzling to have a recipe that calls for 5 cups of shredded cabbage, but says nothing about how much you should buy to get 5 cups. Refer to this handy chart when you're looking for yields of common vegetables.

Asparagus
1 pound = 2 cups cut or snapped
Beans, green
1 pound = 4 cups cut or snapped
Broccoli
1 pound = 6 cups cut broccoli
Cabbage
1 pound = 1 small head, 5 cups raw shredded
Carrots
1 pound = 6 to 8 medium carrots, 3 cups shredded, 2½ cups diced, or 2¼ cups chopped carrots
Cauliflower
1 small head = 4 cups sliced or 3 cups flowerets
Celery
1 medium bunch = 4½ cups chopped

Corn
1 ear = ½ cup cooked kernels
Mushrooms
1 pound = 6 cups whole or sliced
Onions
1 large = 1 cup chopped
1 medium = ½ cup chopped
Pepper, green
1 medium = 1 cup strips or ½ cup chopped
Potatoes
1 pound = 3 medium or 2 cups cubed, cooked
Spinach
1 pound = 12 cups torn
Tomatoes
1 pound = 4 small
12 whole cherry = 1 cup, halved

Fresh Fruit Salads

It's easy to create a fruit salad packed with fresh-picked flavor. You'll see just how easy as you flip through this chapter. Here is an enchanting selection of salads bursting with assorted fruit: juicy apples, tangy oranges, and luscious peaches, to name a few.

In case you're short on time, we've given canned fruit options for convenience. So, what are you waiting for? Start creating.

Ginger Fruit Bowl

Ginger Fruit Bowl

1	medium orange
1	medium apple*
1	medium peach*
½	cup strawberries
¼	cup pineapple yogurt
2	tablespoons mayonnaise *or*
	salad dressing
1	teaspoon brown sugar
¼	teaspoon ground ginger
	Lettuce cups

Working over a small bowl, peel and section orange (see photo 1). Reserve orange juice. Place orange sections in a mixing bowl.

Core apple (see photo 2). Coarsely chop apple; add to bowl. Peel peach (see photo 3). Thinly slice peach (see photo 4). Add peach to bowl. Remove hulls from strawberries (see photo 5). Halve berries; add to bowl. Toss fruit together.

For dressing, in the bowl with reserved orange juice stir together yogurt, mayonnaise or salad dressing, sugar, and ginger. Arrange lettuce cups on 4 individual salad plates. Evenly divide fruit mixture among the plates. Pour dressing over salads. Makes 4 servings.

*To keep cut fruits from turning brown, dip fruit in or brush fruit with a mixture of lemon juice and water or a mixture of water and ascorbic acid color keeper.

1 Using a sharp paring knife, remove the peel and white membrane from the orange.
  Working over a bowl to catch the juices, cut into the center of the fruit between one orange section and the membrane. Turn knife down the other side of the section next to the membrane, as shown.

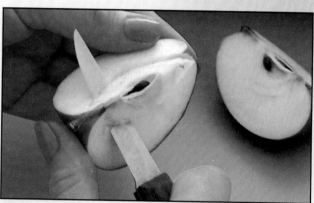

2 Wash the apple. Cut the apple lengthwise in half and then into quarters. Using a paring knife, cut down each side of the apple quarter along the core, as shown. Discard the apple core.

3 Insert a fork into the end of the peach. Dip the peach into boiling water for 20 seconds; remove.

While the peach is still on the fork, peel off the skin with a paring knife. Work from top to bottom, as shown. If the skin doesn't peel easily, return the peach to the boiling water for a few more seconds.

4 Cut the peach lengthwise in half. You don't have to remove the pit; just cut into slices, as shown.

In some peach varieties, plums, and apricots, you can insert the tip of a paring knife near the edge of the pit and gently lift the pit out.

5 Rinse strawberries. Remove strawberry hulls (also called caps) by inserting a paring knife under the hull of each strawberry; lift out the hull. Keep berries at their freshest by washing and hulling just before using them.

Date Waldorf Salad

The original Waldorf Salad was created by the maitre d' of New York's famous Waldorf Astoria Hotel. We've created our own version by adding dates and oranges.

2 medium apples, cored
   (see photo 2, page 20)
1 small orange, peeled and sectioned
   (see photo 1, page 20)
⅓ cup pitted dates, snipped
⅓ cup sliced celery
¼ cup broken walnuts
½ cup frozen whipped dessert topping,
   thawed
¼ cup mayonnaise *or* salad dressing
   Lettuce leaves

Coarsely chop apples. In a medium bowl combine chopped apples, orange sections and reserved orange juice, snipped dates, sliced celery, and broken walnuts.

For dressing, in a small bowl combine thawed whipped dessert topping and mayonnaise or salad dressing. Spoon dressing over fruit mixture. Toss to coat. Line a serving bowl with lettuce leaves. Spoon salad into the bowl. Makes 6 servings.

Cranberry-Pear Salad

2 medium pears, cored (see photo 2,
   page 20)
1 medium orange, peeled and sectioned
   (see photo 1, page 20)
½ cup seedless green grapes, halved
½ of an 8-ounce can (½ cup) whole
   cranberry sauce

Coarsely chop pears. In a medium bowl combine chopped pears, orange sections, and halved grapes.

For dressing, in a small bowl stir together reserved orange juice and cranberry sauce. Pour dressing over fruit mixture. Toss to coat. Makes 4 servings.

Three-Fruit Salad

Choose your favorite honey for this delightful dressing. The source of the bees' flower pollen determines the taste, color, and thickness of the honey.

2 medium peaches, peeled and sliced
   (see photos 3–4, page 21)
1 medium grapefruit, peeled and
   sectioned (see photo 1, page 20)
1 cup strawberries, hulled
   (see photo 5, page 21)
¼ cup honey
1 tablespoon lemon juice
½ teaspoon poppy seed
   Spinach leaves (optional)

In a bowl combine the sliced peaches, grapefruit sections, and strawberries.

For dressing, in a small bowl stir together honey, lemon juice, and poppy seed. Pour dressing over fruit mixture. Toss to coat. If desired, serve on a bed of spinach leaves. Makes 4 servings.

Easy Apricot Salad

Toast almonds by placing them in a 9-inch pie plate. Bake in a 350° oven for 10 to 12 minutes, stirring once during baking.

4 apricots, peeled and pitted (see photos 3–4, page 21), *or* one 8¾-ounce can apricot halves, drained
1 small apple, cored (see photo 2, page 20)
   Lemon juice
1 8-ounce can pineapple chunks, drained
⅓ cup thinly sliced celery
¼ cup slivered almonds, toasted
⅓ cup dairy sour cream
1 tablespoon apricot preserves *or* orange marmalade
1 teaspoon lemon juice
¼ teaspoon ground nutmeg
2 cups torn lettuce *or* salad greens

Cut apricots into bite-size pieces. Coarsely chop apple. In a bowl combine apricots and apple. Sprinkle with lemon juice; toss to coat. Stir in pineapple, celery, and almonds.

For dressing, in a small bowl combine sour cream, preserves or marmalade, 1 teaspoon lemon juice, and nutmeg.

Before serving, pour dressing over fruit mixture. Add lettuce or salad greens; toss to coat. Makes 4 to 6 servings.

Plum-Banana Salad

4 plums, pitted (see photo 4, page 21)
1 medium nectarine, peeled (see photo 3, page 21)
2 firm medium bananas
2 tablespoons lemon juice
¼ cup orange marmalade
2 teaspoons salad oil
¼ teaspoon poppy seed

Slice plums. Coarsely chop nectarine. Peel and bias-slice bananas. In a large bowl combine plums, nectarine, and bananas. Sprinkle with lemon juice; toss to coat.

For dressing, in a small bowl stir together orange marmalade, salad oil, and poppy seed. Pour dressing over fruit mixture. Toss to coat. Makes 4 servings.

Cool Down

Try one of these cooling tips to make any of the salads in this chapter refreshingly cold.

● Chill ingredients thoroughly before you make the salad.

● Prepare the salad, cover, and chill for at least 1 hour.

● For a quick cool down, place the salad, covered, in your freezer for 20 minutes.

Super-Simple Main Dishes

With a flick of the wrists, these salads are ready. You can turn everyday egg salad into tantalizing Avocado and Egg Salad. Or, change humdrum ham salad into tropical Ham-Pineapple Salad.

Fix and feast in minutes or prepare your favorite salad ahead and chill till you're ready for a delectable dinner.

Broccoli-Salmon Salad

Broccoli-Salmon Salad

1   15½-ounce can salmon
1   cup small broccoli *or* cauliflower
      flowerets (see photo 2, page 14)
½   cup thinly sliced radishes
½   cup chopped celery
¼   cup mayonnaise *or* salad dressing
¼   cup dairy sour cream
1   tablespoon sweet pickle relish
1   tablespoon milk
⅛   teaspoon pepper
      Romaine leaves

Drain salmon. Remove skin and bones; discard (see photo 1). Set salmon aside. In a large bowl combine broccoli or cauliflower, radishes, and celery (see photo 2).

For dressing, in a small bowl stir together mayonnaise or salad dressing, sour cream, pickle relish, milk, and pepper (see photo 3). Pour dressing over vegetable mixture. Toss to coat. Gently stir in salmon. Line 4 plates with romaine leaves (see photo 4). Spoon salad onto plates. Makes 4 main-dish servings.

2 Add the sliced celery to the other vegetables. All the vegetables, but not the salmon, are added at this time. The salmon is added after the vegetables and dressing are combined. Adding the salmon last keeps it in large bite-size chunks.

1 Using your fingers, separate the canned salmon into sections. Carefully remove the skin, bone, and cartilage; discard. Break the salmon into large chunks; set aside.

3 Combine dressing ingredients in a separate bowl. Thoroughly mix the ingredients before adding dressing to the salad.

4 Arrange romaine leaves on one side of the dinner plate, as shown. If you're using an individual salad plate, arrange leaves in the center and around the edges of the plate. The leaves add both color and crunch to the salad.

Confetti Tuna Salad

1 9¼-ounce can tuna, drained and flaked
1 cup shredded carrot (see photo 4, page 15)
1 cup sliced celery
2 tablespoons finely chopped onion
⅓ cup plain yogurt
2 teaspoons prepared mustard
¼ teaspoon pepper
¼ cup chopped pecans *or* peanuts
Torn salad greens

In a large bowl combine tuna, carrot, celery, and onion (see photo 2, page 26). For dressing, in a small bowl stir together yogurt, mustard, and pepper (see photo 3, page 27). Pour dressing over tuna mixture. Toss to coat.

Before serving, fold in chopped pecans or peanuts. Arrange torn greens on 4 individual salad plates. Spoon salad onto greens. Makes 4 main-dish servings.

Ham-Pineapple Salad

1 8-ounce can crushed pineapple (juice pack)
2 cups cubed fully cooked ham
½ cup seedless red *or* green grapes, halved
¼ cup chopped green pepper
½ cup plain yogurt
¼ teaspoon ground cinnamon
Dash ground nutmeg
Lettuce *or* spinach leaves

Drain pineapple, reserving *2 tablespoons* pineapple juice. In a large bowl combine drained pineapple, ham, grapes, and green pepper (see photo 2, page 26).

For dressing, in a small bowl stir together reserved pineapple juice, yogurt, cinnamon, and nutmeg (see photo 3, page 27). Pour dressing over ham mixture. Toss to coat. Line a serving bowl with lettuce or spinach leaves; spoon salad into bowl. Makes 4 main-dish servings.

Cheesy Shrimp Salad

Personalize this recipe—substitute your favorite kind of cheese for the cheddar and Monterey Jack.

4 ounces cheddar cheese, cubed (1 cup)
4 ounces Monterey Jack cheese, cubed (1 cup)
1 cup sliced celery
1 4½-ounce can shrimp, rinsed and drained
½ cup chopped green pepper
¾ cup sour cream dip with toasted onion
1 tablespoon milk
¼ teaspoon dried basil, crushed
⅓ cup broken walnuts
Lettuce leaves

In a medium bowl combine cheddar cheese, Monterey Jack cheese, celery, shrimp, and green pepper (see photo 2, page 26).

For dressing, in a small bowl stir together sour cream dip, milk, and basil (see photo 3, page 27). Pour dressing over cheese-shrimp mixture. Toss to coat.

Before serving, stir in walnuts. Line a serving bowl with lettuce; spoon salad into bowl. Makes 4 main-dish servings.

Fruited Chicken Salad

If you don't have cooked chicken on hand, substitute frozen diced cooked chicken. Just thaw it and use as you would cooked chicken.

 2 **medium peaches, peeled and pitted
     (see photos 3–4, page 21), *or*
     1 cup frozen sliced peaches, thawed**
 2 **cups cubed cooked chicken**
 1 **cup pitted dark sweet cherries *or*
     seedless red grapes**
 ½ **cup sliced celery**
 ½ **cup mayonnaise *or* salad dressing**
 ½ **teaspoon curry powder**
 ⅛ **teaspoon salt**
 2 **firm large bananas**
 1 **tablespoon water**
 1 **tablespoon lemon juice**
     Leaf lettuce
 ½ **cup cashews *or* peanuts**
     Coconut, toasted (optional)

Cut peaches into bite-size pieces. In a large bowl combine peaches, chicken, cherries or grapes, and celery (see photo 2, page 26).

For dressing, in a small bowl stir together mayonnaise or salad dressing, curry powder, and salt (see photo 3, page 27). Pour dressing over chicken mixture. Toss to coat.

Just before serving, slice bananas. In a small bowl combine water and lemon juice. Add bananas; toss gently to coat. Arrange lettuce on 4 individual salad plates (see photo 4, page 27). Arrange bananas on top of lettuce leaves.

Stir cashews or peanuts into chicken mixture. Place *one-fourth* of the chicken mixture atop bananas on each plate. Sprinkle with toasted coconut, if desired. Makes 4 main-dish servings.

Avocado and Egg Salad

Have your hard-cooked eggs ever had a greenish ring around the yolk? You'll reduce the chance of getting these rings by carefully watching the cooking time. When the eggs are done, immediately place them in cold water.

 6 **hard-cooked eggs**
 1 **large avocado, peeled and cut into cubes**
 1 **tablespoon lemon juice**
 ½ **cup chopped celery**
 1 **tablespoon sliced green onion**
 ⅓ **cup mayonnaise *or* salad dressing**
 1½ **teaspoons prepared mustard**
 ¼ **teaspoon salt**
 ⅛ **teaspoon pepper**
     Lettuce cups (optional)
 2 **slices bacon, crisp-cooked,
     drained, and crumbled**

Peel and coarsely chop eggs. In a large bowl combine avocado and lemon juice; toss. Add eggs, celery, and onion (see photo 2, page 26).

For dressing, in a small bowl combine mayonnaise or salad dressing, mustard, salt, and pepper (see photo 3, page 27). Pour dressing over egg mixture. Toss to coat.

To serve, spoon salad into individual lettuce cups, if desired. Sprinkle crumbled bacon on top. Makes 3 main-dish servings.

Frosty Fruit Salads

When you want something cold and refreshing, think of a frosty frozen salad. These super salads can work double-duty, too. Consider using them for a side-dish salad or as an enticing dessert.

Just mix up your favorite frozen salad and slide it into the freezer. The next time you're in the mood for something cool and creamy to soothe you, reach for a frosty salad.

Avocado Fruit Freeze

Avocado Fruit Freeze

Loaded with oodles of cream cheese and sour cream, this salad says "creamy"!

1 **avocado, halved, seeded, and peeled**
1 **tablespoon lemon juice**
1 **8-ounce can jellied cranberry sauce**
1 **3-ounce package cream cheese**
⅓ **cup dairy sour cream**
¼ **cup sugar**
1 **8-ounce can crushed pineapple (juice pack), drained**
  Leaf lettuce

Chop avocado. In a bowl combine avocado and lemon juice; toss. Chop about *half* of the jellied cranberry sauce. Reserve remainder for garnish.

In a small mixer bowl combine cream cheese, sour cream, and sugar. Beat with an electric mixer till smooth. Fold in avocado, chopped cranberry sauce, and drained pineapple (see photo 1). Transfer mixture to a 9x5x3-inch loaf pan (see photo 2). Cover and freeze 6 hours or till firm.

To serve, let salad stand at room temperature about 20 minutes to thaw slightly. Line 6 individual salad plates with leaf lettuce. Cut salad lengthwise in half, then crosswise to make 6 equal pieces (see photo 3). Remove with spatula to salad plates. Slice remaining cranberry sauce and cut into attractive shapes to garnish salads (see photo 4). Makes 6 servings.

Frosty Circles: Prepare Avocado Fruit Freeze as above. Spoon mixture into two 12-ounce or four 6-ounce juice concentrate cans. Cover and freeze. Let stand at room temperature about 20 minutes to thaw slightly. To remove salads, open bottom end of can and push salad out. Cut into 1-inch-thick slices. Serve as directed.

1 Gently fold the avocado, cranberry sauce, and pineapple into the beaten cream cheese mixture. Stir thoroughly to combine all the ingredients.

2 Transfer the mixture to a 9x5x3-inch loaf pan. Using a rubber spatula or the back of a wooden spoon, spread the mixture evenly in the pan. Cover with foil or plastic wrap.

3 Remove the salad from the freezer about 20 minutes before serving. This standing time allows the salad to thaw slightly so it's easier to cut. Using a sharp knife, cut the salad into squares.

4 Garnish each salad with the remaining cranberry sauce. Use small cookie cutters or other small cutters to cut shapes from the cranberry sauce. Place the shapes on top of each salad.

Frosty Tropical Salads

Present this festive salad as either a side-dish salad or as a dessert.

  1 **8-ounce container soft-style cream cheese with pineapple**
  ½ **cup whipping cream**
  2 **medium bananas, peeled and chopped**
  1 **8-ounce can crushed pineapple (juice pack)**
  ½ **cup maraschino cherries, finely chopped**
  ¼ **cup chopped nuts**
     Lettuce leaves

In a small mixer bowl beat soft-style cream cheese with an electric mixer on medium speed for 30 seconds. Gradually add whipping cream, beating till fluffy.

Stir in chopped bananas, *undrained* pineapple, cherries, and nuts (see photo 1). Transfer fruit mixture to a 9x5x3-inch loaf pan (see photo 2). Cover and freeze 6 hours or till firm.

To serve, let salad stand at room temperature about 20 minutes to thaw slightly. Line 8 individual salad plates with lettuce leaves. Cut salad lengthwise in half, then crosswise to make 4 equal slices (see photo 3). Remove with a spatula to salad plates. Makes 8 servings.

Marinated Side-Dish Salads

You'll understand the saying "Great things come to those who wait" as soon as you sample these marinated side-dish salads. These salads let time work in your favor. Marinating them allows each salad to absorb the unique flavors of the marinade.

So, the next time you pack a picnic, take along Three-Bean Carrot Salad. Or, serve showy Marinated Mushrooms to those special dinner guests.

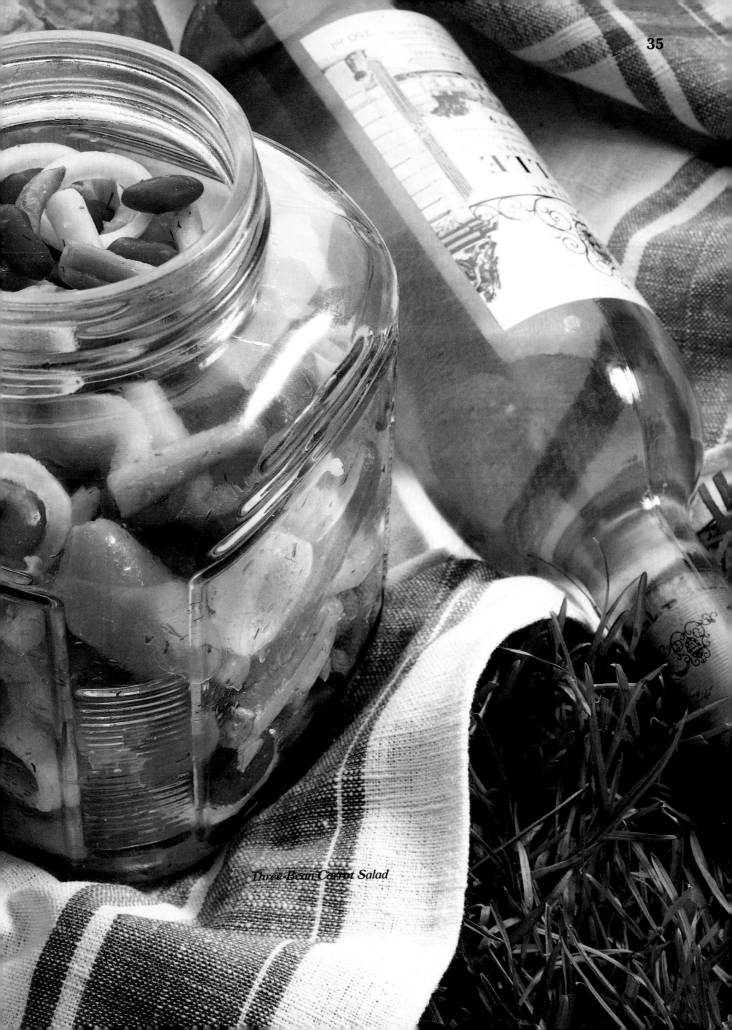

Three-Bean Carrot Salad

Three-Bean Carrot Salad

1 8¼-ounce can small whole carrots, drained
1 8-ounce can cut wax beans, drained
1 8-ounce can cut green beans, drained
1 8-ounce can red kidney beans, drained
1 small onion, sliced and separated into rings
1 small green pepper, seeded and sliced into rings
⅔ cup vinegar
½ cup salad oil
2 tablespoons sugar
½ teaspoon dried dillweed *or* 1 teaspoon dried savory, crushed
1 clove garlic, minced
  Lettuce leaves (optional)

In a large bowl combine carrots, wax beans, green beans, kidney beans, onion rings, and green pepper rings.

For marinade, in a screw-top jar combine vinegar, salad oil, sugar, dillweed or savory, and minced garlic. Cover and shake well (see photo 1). Pour marinade over vegetables (see photo 2). Cover and chill 2 to 24 hours, stirring occasionally (see photo 3).

Line a bowl with lettuce leaves, if desired. Using a slotted spoon, remove vegetables from marinade to a bowl or a serving container (see photo 4). Makes 6 servings.

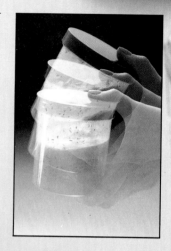

1 Combine the marinade ingredients in a screw-top jar. (A screw-top jar works best because you can shake it without spilling). Shake the jar well to thoroughly combine the ingredients.

2 Pour the marinade over the vegetables. Use a spoon to stir the mixture and evenly coat all the vegetables.

3 Stir the vegetables occasionally during the marinating time. This helps to distribute the marinade and to coat all the ingredients.

4 To serve, use a large, slotted spoon to remove the vegetables from the marinade. The slots in the spoon allow the liquid to drain off of the vegetables.

Marinated Mushrooms

3 cups fresh mushrooms, sliced (8 ounces)
¼ cup white wine vinegar
1 small onion, thinly sliced
¼ cup chopped green pepper
2 tablespoons water
2 tablespoons salad oil
1 tablespoon Dijon-style mustard
¼ teaspoon salt
¼ teaspoon dried basil, crushed
⅛ teaspoon pepper
1½ cups coarsely shredded zucchini, carrot, *or* lettuce

In a bowl toss mushrooms with vinegar. Add onion and green pepper.

For marinade, in a screw-top jar combine water, oil, mustard, salt, basil, and pepper. Cover and shake well (see photo 1, page 36). Pour marinade over vegetables (see photo 2, page 36). Cover and chill 2 to 24 hours, stirring occasionally (see photo 3, page 36).

Divide shredded zucchini, carrot, or lettuce among 4 individual salad plates. Using a slotted spoon, remove vegetables from marinade to salad plates, reserving marinade (see photo 4, page 37). Drizzle about *1 tablespoon* of reserved marinade over each salad. Serves 4.

Caraway Cabbage Salad

5 cups shredded cabbage
   (see photo 1, page 14)
1 2-ounce jar sliced pimiento, drained
¼ cup sliced green onion
¼ cup chopped green pepper
⅓ cup vinegar
¼ cup salad oil
2 tablespoons water
1 teaspoon sugar
½ teaspoon caraway seed
¼ teaspoon salt
¼ teaspoon dried marjoram, crushed
⅛ teaspoon pepper
Parsley sprigs (optional)

In a large bowl combine cabbage, pimiento, green onion, and green pepper.

For marinade, in a screw-top jar combine vinegar, salad oil, water, sugar, caraway seed, salt, marjoram, and pepper. Cover and shake well (see photo 1, page 36). Pour marinade over vegetables (see photo 2, page 36). Cover and chill 2 to 24 hours, stirring occasionally (see photo 3, page 36).

Using a slotted spoon, remove vegetables from marinade and place in a serving bowl (see photo 4, page 37). Garnish with parsley sprigs, if desired. Makes 6 servings.

Spiced Fruit Salad

Although allspice smells like a delicious combination of cinnamon, nutmeg, and cloves, the spice actually comes from the berry of an evergreen tree.

1 small pear, cored (see photo 2, page 20)
2 medium peaches, peeled, pitted, and sliced (see photos 3–4, page 21)
½ cup orange juice
2 tablespoons honey
¼ teaspoon ground cinnamon
Dash ground allspice
Lettuce leaves (optional)
1 cup strawberries, hulled and halved (see photo 5, page 21)
1 kiwi fruit, peeled and sliced, *or* ½ cup seedless green grapes, halved

Cut pear into large pieces. In a large bowl combine pear pieces and sliced peaches.

For marinade, in a screw-top jar combine orange juice, honey, cinnamon, and allspice. Cover and shake well (see photo 1, page 36). Pour marinade over fruit (see photo 2, page 36). Cover and chill 2 to 24 hours, stirring occasionally (see photo 3, page 36).

Before serving, line a serving bowl with lettuce leaves, if desired. Gently stir strawberries and kiwi fruit or grapes into marinated fruit. Using a slotted spoon, remove fruit from marinade to the lettuce-lined bowl, reserving marinade (see photo 4, page 37). Pour *¼ cup* of the reserved marinade over fruit. Makes 4 servings.

Dilled Vegetable Combo

1 cup thinly sliced zucchini
1 cup sliced cauliflower flowerets (see photo 2, page 14)
2 small carrots, cut into julienne strips (see tip box, page 15))
2 tablespoons sliced green onion
2 tablespoons snipped parsley
¼ cup white wine vinegar
¼ cup salad oil
1 teaspoon dried dillweed *or* ½ teaspoon dried savory, crushed
½ teaspoon celery seed
¼ teaspoon salt
⅛ teaspoon pepper
Leaf lettuce
1 6-ounce package frozen pea pods, thawed
Snipped parlsey (optional)

In a bowl combine zucchini, cauliflower, carrots, onion, and 2 tablespoons snipped parsley.

For marinade, in a screw-top jar combine vinegar, salad oil, dillweed or savory, celery seed, salt, and pepper. Cover and shake well (see photo 1, page 36). Pour marinade over vegetables (see photo 2, page 36). Cover and chill 2 to 24 hours, stirring occasionally (see photo 3, page 36).

Line a platter with leaf lettuce. Before serving, stir thawed pea pods into vegetables. Using a slotted spoon, remove vegetables from marinade to the lettuce-lined platter (see photo 4, page 37). Sprinkle snipped parsley over salad, if desired. Makes 6 servings.

24-Hour Layered Salads

Fix and forget. These salads can be made and stored up to 24 hours before mealtime. Just prepare the salad ingredients and layer them. Then seal out the air and lock in the freshness with a creamy dressing. When you're ready to serve, the salad looks and tastes as fresh as if you just made it—greens and all.

Just toss it together or serve it in layers. From first forkful to last bite, all of these salads stack up!

All-American Layered Salad

All-American Layered Salad

Our version of this American picnic and potluck favorite has a delicate dill dressing capped by shredded cheddar cheese and tiny bits of ham.

4 cups torn salad greens (see pages 8–9)
1 cup shredded carrot (see photo 4, page 15)
¼ cup sliced green onion
1 cup frozen peas
1 cup mayonnaise *or* salad dressing
2 tablespoons milk
½ teaspoon dried dillweed
¾ cup shredded cheddar cheese (3 ounces)
¼ cup finely chopped fully cooked ham

In the bottom of a medium bowl place torn greens (see photo 1). Layer in the following order: shredded carrot, green onion, and frozen peas (see photo 2).

For dressing, in a small bowl combine mayonnaise or salad dressing, milk, and dillweed. Spread dressing evenly over top of salad (see photo 3). Sprinkle with cheese and ham. Cover tightly with clear plastic wrap (see photo 4). Chill up to 24 hours. Makes 4 servings.

1 Arrange the greens in an even layer in the bottom of the bowl. The greens are put in the bottom of the bowl to keep excess moisture away from the vegetables and dressing.

2 Layer the remaining ingredients in the bowl: first the shredded carrot, then the green onion, and finally the frozen peas. Try to keep the layers as even as possible. As the salad chills in the refrigerator, the peas will thaw.

3 Using a rubber spatula or knife, spread the dressing evenly over the pea layer, sealing the dressing to the edge of the bowl. The dressing layer helps seal out air, keeping the salad crisp and fresh.

4 Cover the salad tightly with clear plastic wrap before chilling. This prevents the dressing from drying out and keeps the ham and cheese fresh. Ingredients that might become soggy or discolored are sprinkled on just before serving.

Curried Fruit Salad

Using the purchased fruit bits is a real timesaver—they're already cut up .

1 8¼-ounce can crushed pineapple
6 cups torn salad greens (see pages 8–9)
1 6-ounce package mixed dried fruit bits
¾ cup thinly sliced celery
1 11-ounce can mandarin orange sections, drained
½ cup orange yogurt
¼ teaspoon curry powder
1 medium banana, sliced
¼ cup coarsely chopped cashews

Drain pineapple, reserving ¼ cup of the juice; set aside.

In the bottom of a large bowl or 3-quart casserole place *half* of the greens (see photo 1, page 42). Layer in the following order: dried fruit bits, celery, orange sections, remaining greens, and pineapple (see photo 2, page 42).

For dressing, in a small bowl combine reserved pineapple juice, orange yogurt, and curry powder. Spread dressing evenly over top of salad (see photo 3, page 43). Cover tightly with clear plastic wrap (see photo 4, page 43). Chill up to 24 hours.

Before serving, arrange sliced banana on top of salad. Sprinkle with chopped cashews. Serve immediately. Makes 4 to 6 servings.

Layered Reuben Salad

Use rye melba toast to enjoy all the flavors of a hearty reuben sandwich.

2 cups finely shredded cabbage (see photo 1, page 14)
2 cups finely shredded lettuce (see pages 8–9)
1 8-ounce bottle Thousand Island salad dressing
1 teaspoon caraway seed
2 3-ounce packages sliced corned beef, chopped
3 hard-cooked eggs, sliced
1 cup shredded Swiss cheese (4 ounces)
4 slices melba toast, coarsely crushed

In a mixing bowl combine cabbage, lettuce, ¼ cup of the Thousand Island salad dressing, and caraway seed. In the bottom of a medium bowl or an 8x8x2-inch dish place *half* of the cabbage mixture (see photo 1, page 42). Layer in the following order: *half* of the corned beef, remaining cabbage mixture, remaining corned beef, hard-cooked egg slices, and shredded cheese (see photo 2, page 42).

Spread remaining Thousand Island salad dressing evenly over top of salad (see photo 3, page 43). Cover tightly with clear plastic wrap (see photo 4, page 43). Chill up to 24 hours. Before serving, top with crushed melba toast. Makes 4 main-dish servings.

Greek Layered Salad

We liked the color contrast between the spinach and iceberg lettuce, but any salad greens you have on hand will work.

 3 cups torn spinach (see pages 8–9)
 3 cups torn lettuce (see pages 8–9)
 ½ cup sliced pitted ripe olives
 1 cup alfalfa sprouts
 1 cup cherry tomatoes, quartered, *or*
     1 cup chopped tomato
 1 cup crumbled feta cheese (4 ounces)
 1 8-ounce carton plain yogurt
 1 small cucumber, shredded
 ¼ teaspoon garlic salt
 ¼ teaspoon dried oregano, crushed

In a bowl combine spinach and lettuce. In the bottom of a medium salad bowl or a 12x7x2-inch dish place *half* of the greens (see photo 1, page 42). Reserve *2 tablespoons* sliced olives; set aside. Layer in the following order: remaining olives, alfalfa sprouts, tomatoes, feta cheese, and remaining greens (see photo 2, page 42).

For dressing, in a small bowl combine yogurt, cucumber, garlic salt, and oregano. Spread dressing evenly over top of salad (see photo 3, page 43). Cover tightly with clear plastic wrap (see photo 4, page 43). Chill up to 24 hours. Before serving, garnish with reserved sliced olives. Makes 8 servings.

Fiesta Salad

Tiny bits of fiery peppers in the Monterey Jack cheese add a spunky hotness to this salad.

 3 cups torn salad greens (see pages 8–9)
 1 8-ounce can kidney beans, rinsed and
     well drained
 1 cup shredded Monterey Jack cheese
     with jalapeño peppers (4 ounces)
 1 large tomato, seeded and chopped
 ⅓ cup sliced pitted ripe olives
 1 8-ounce container sour cream dip with
     avocado (1 cup)
    Several dashes bottled hot pepper sauce
 ¾ cup slightly crushed corn chips

In the bottom of a medium bowl or an 8x8x2-inch dish place *2 cups* of greens (see photo 1, page 42). Layer in the following order: beans, cheese, remaining greens, tomato, and olives (see photo 2, page 42).

For dressing, in a small bowl combine sour cream dip and bottled hot pepper sauce.

Spread dressing evenly over top of salad (see photo 3, page 43). Cover tightly with clear plastic wrap (see photo 4, page 43). Chill up to 24 hours. Before serving, sprinkle with crushed corn chips. Makes 6 servings.

Grape and Pineapple Salad

2 cups shredded *or* torn salad greens (see pages 8–9)
1½ cups seedless red *or* green grapes, halved
1 8-ounce can pineapple tidbits (juice pack), well drained
½ of a 4-ounce container frozen whipped dessert topping, thawed
½ cup plain yogurt
⅛ teaspoon ground cinnamon
⅓ cup flaked coconut, toasted

In the bottom of a small bowl or 1½-quart casserole place greens (see photo 1, page 42). Layer grapes and pineapple (see photo 2, page 42).

For dressing, in a small bowl combine dessert topping, yogurt, and cinnamon. Spread dressing evenly over top of salad (see photo 3, page 43). Cover tightly with clear plastic wrap (see photo 4, page 43). Chill up to 24 hours. Before serving, sprinkle with coconut. Serves 6.

Apple-Orange Salad

2 medium apples, cored (see photo 2, page 20)
2 tablespoons lemon juice
5 cups torn salad greens
1 11-ounce can mandarin orange sections, drained
1 3-ounce package cream cheese, softened
3 tablespoons orange *or* pineapple juice
Salted sunflower nuts

Cut apples into thin wedges, then toss with lemon juice. In the bottom of a 1½-quart serving bowl place *half* of the torn greens (see photo 1, page 42). Layer in the following order: *half* of the mandarin orange sections, remaining greens, and apple slices (see photo 2, page 42).

For dressing, in a small mixer bowl beat softened cream cheese with an electric mixer till smooth. Add orange or pineapple juice gradually while beating. Spread dressing evenly over top of salad (see photo 3, page 43) Arrange remaining orange sections on top. Cover tightly with clear plastic wrap (see photo 4, page 43). Chill up to 24 hours. Before serving, sprinkle with sunflower nuts. Makes 4 or 5 servings.

Chicken and Curry Salad

4 cups shredded salad greens (see pages 8–9)
2 cups cubed cooked chicken (10 ounces)
½ cup raisins
¼ cup sliced green onion
½ cup thinly sliced celery
¾ cup mayonnaise *or* salad dressing
1 tablespoon chutney
½ teaspoon curry powder
¼ teaspoon paprika
Dash garlic salt
¼ cup dry roasted peanuts, coarsely chopped

In the bottom of a medium bowl place *half* of the shredded greens (see photo 1, page 42). Layer in the following order: chicken, raisins, green onion, celery, and remaining greens (see photo 2, page 42).

For dressing, in a small bowl combine mayonnaise or salad dressing, chutney, curry powder, paprika, and garlic salt. Spread dressing evenly over top of salad (see photo 3, page 43). Cover tightly with clear plastic wrap (see photo 4, page 43). Chill up to 24 hours. Before serving, sprinkle with peanuts. Makes 4 main-dish servings.

◄ *Pictured opposite: Chicken and Curry Salad*

Savory Vegetable Salads

Don't just dream of creamy potato salad, spunky bean salad, or any other vegetable salad favorite. Make yourself some! You'll love eating your vegetables when they're tucked in a tasty salad. They're truly irresistible!

Begin your salad with a savvy selection of vegetables, cooked to perfection. Then choose your dressing from a variety of tempting toppings. It's all designed to bring out the vegetable lover in you.

Italian Bean and Potato Salad

Italian Bean and Potato Salad

8 to 10 tiny new potatoes (1 pound)
1 9-ounce package frozen Italian
    green beans
1 cup sliced fresh mushrooms *or* one
    2½-ounce jar sliced mushrooms,
    drained
⅓ cup bottled Italian salad dressing
¼ cup sliced green onion
3 slices bacon, crisp-cooked, drained,
    and crumbled, *or* 2 ounces prosciutto,
    chopped
2 tablespoons grated Parmesan cheese

In a saucepan cook potatoes, covered, in boiling lightly salted water about 20 minutes or till tender (see photo 1). Drain; cool slightly. Cut potatoes into bite-size pieces (see photo 2).

Meanwhile, in a small saucepan cook green beans and fresh mushrooms according to package directions just till beans are crisp-tender (see photo 3). Drain.

In a large bowl combine potatoes, green beans, mushrooms, salad dressing, and green onion. Cover and chill 2 to 24 hours. Before serving, sprinkle with bacon or prosciutto and Parmesan cheese (see photo 4). Serves 4.

1 Carefully insert a fork into one of the potatoes. If it's difficult to pierce the potato, the potato needs further cooking. When you can insert and remove the fork easily, the potato is tender.

2 Let the potatoes cool slightly. When they're cool enough to handle, place them on a cutting board. Cut each potato into small bite-size pieces. Leaving the peel on these tiny new potatoes adds vitamins and fiber, but whether to peel the potatoes is your decision.

3 Save yourself time and energy by cooking the green beans and fresh mushrooms together. Test the green beans by removing a bean from the saucepan; cool slightly. Bite into the bean. Beans should be tender, but still crisp. This stage is called *crisp-tender.*

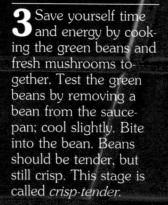

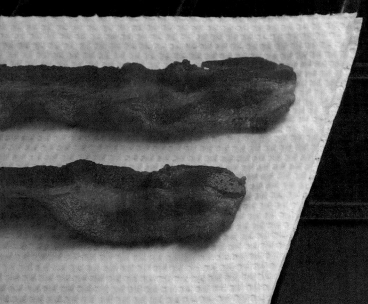

4 Just before serving, sprinkle bacon pieces and Parmesan cheese over the salad. Adding these just prior to serving helps keep the bacon crisp and the cheese fresh.

Dilled Vegetable Vinaigrette

2 tablespoons water
2 tablespoons vinegar
2 tablespoons olive oil *or* salad oil
1 teaspoon sugar
1 teaspoon dried dillweed
¼ teaspoon dried savory, crushed
3 cups sliced fresh mushrooms (8 ounces)
2 medium carrots, cut into julienne strips
   (see tip box, page 15)
½ cup thinly sliced celery
2 medium tomatoes, sliced
4 leaves leaf lettuce *or* romaine

In a large saucepan combine water, vinegar, olive or salad oil, sugar, dillweed, and savory. Add mushrooms, carrots, and celery. Bring to boiling; reduce heat. Cover and simmer 5 minutes or till vegetables are crisp-tender (see photo 3, page 50). Pour vegetable mixture into a bowl. Cover and chill 2 to 24 hours.

Before serving, arrange tomato slices on 4 lettuce-lined salad plates. Using a slotted spoon, place *one-fourth* of the vegetable mixture on each plate, reserving vinaigrette mixture. Drizzle salads with vinaigrette mixture. Serves 4.

Creamy Potato Salad

6 medium potatoes (2 pounds)
1 cup thinly sliced celery
½ cup finely chopped onion
⅓ cup chopped sweet pickle
1¼ cups mayonnaise *or* salad dressing
2 teaspoons sugar
2 teaspoons celery seed
2 teaspoons vinegar
2 teaspoons prepared mustard
2 hard-cooked eggs, coarsely chopped

In a saucepan cook potatoes, covered, in boiling lightly salted water about 25 minutes or till-tender (see photo 1, page 50). Drain; cool slightly. Using a paring knife, peel potatoes. Cut into bite-size pieces (see photo 2, page 50).

In a large bowl combine potatoes, celery, onion, and sweet pickle. For dressing, in a small bowl combine mayonnaise or salad dressing, sugar, celery seed, vinegar, prepared mustard, and 1½ teaspoons *salt*. Pour dressing over potato mixture. Toss to coat. Carefully fold in chopped eggs. Cover and chill 2 to 24 hours. Serves 8.

Sweet Potato and Pecan Salad

"Y'all come and get it!" Here's a Southern-style salad made with sweet potatoes and toasted pecans, and tossed with a delicate orange dressing.

1 pound sweet potatoes
1 3-ounce package cream cheese, softened
¼ cup snipped parsley
½ teaspoon salt
¼ teaspoon finely shredded orange peel
⅛ teaspoon pepper
¼ cup orange juice
½ cup thinly sliced celery
½ cup chopped pecans, toasted

Cut large sweet potatoes into 2 or 3 pieces. In a saucepan cook sweet potatoes, covered, in boiling lightly salted water about 25 minutes or till tender (see photo 1, page 50). Drain; cool slightly. Using a paring knife, peel potatoes. Cut potatoes into bite-size pieces (see photo 2, page 50).

In a large bowl combine cream cheese, parsley, salt, orange peel, and pepper. Stir in orange juice, then mix well. Add potato pieces, celery, and pecans. Toss to coat. Cover and chill 2 to 24 hours. Stir gently before serving. Serves 4.

Perky Potato Salad

3 medium potatoes (1 pound)
¼ cup snipped parsley
¼ cup olive oil *or* salad oil
3 tablespoons lemon juice
2 tablespoons thinly sliced green onion
¼ teaspoon salt
⅛ teaspoon garlic powder
Several dashes bottled hot pepper sauce
Dash pepper

In a saucepan cook potatoes, covered, in boiling lightly salted water about 25 minutes or till tender (see photo 1, page 50). Drain; cool slightly. Using a paring knife, peel potatoes. Cut potatoes into bite-size pieces (see photo 2, page 50).

In a bowl combine parsley, olive or salad oil, lemon juice, green onion, salt, garlic powder, hot pepper sauce, and pepper. Add potato pieces. Toss to coat. Cover and chill 2 to 24 hours. Makes 4 or 5 servings.

Tater Salad

3 medium potatoes (1 pound)
⅓ cup sweet pickle juice
2 teaspoons prepared mustard
½ cup chopped red *or* green pepper
2 hard-cooked eggs, chopped
¼ cup thinly sliced sweet pickle
3 tablespoons chopped green onion

In a saucepan cook potatoes, covered, in boiling lightly salted water about 25 minutes or till tender (see photo 1, page 50). Drain; cool slightly. Using a paring knife, peel potatoes. Cut into bite-size pieces (see photo 2, page 50).

In a large bowl combine pickle juice and prepared mustard. Add potato pieces, ½ cup red or green pepper, eggs, ¼ cup sweet pickles, and green onion. Toss to coat. Cover and chill 2 to 24 hours. Garnish with pickled pepper strips and pickle slices, if desired. Makes 5 servings.

Delectable Vegetables

Next time you're ready to start cooking vegetables, think micro-cooking. Both quick and easy, it's a great way to cook vegetables. Wash and trim vegetables (peel, if necessary). Place in a nonmetal dish or casserole; add 2 tablespoons *water*.

Broccoli spears (1 pound)
   5 to 7 minutes
Broccoli cuts, ½-inch pieces (1 pound)
   6 to 8 minutes
Carrots, ¼-inch slices (1 pound)
   7 to 9 minutes
Celery, chopped (1 cup)
   5 to 7 minutes
Mushrooms, sliced (½ pound)
   2½ to 3½ minutes

Cover with a lid or vented clear plastic wrap. Micro-cook on 100% (HIGH) power for length of time indicated on chart. Stir or rearrange the vegetables once during cooking (stir zucchini twice). All timings are for 600- to 700-watt microwave ovens.

Onions, ¼-inch slices (½ pound)
   4 to 6 minutes
Peppers, green, chopped (½ cup)
   1½ to 3 minutes
Potatoes, quartered (1½ pounds)
   12 to 15 minutes
Potatoes, new whole (¾ pound)
   6 to 8 minutes
Zucchini squash, ¼-inch slices (1 pound)
   6 to 8 minutes

Blue Cheese Garden Salad

Rich and creamy describes this spectacular salad dressing, made with whipped cream and chunks of blue cheese.

1½ **cups thinly sliced carrots**
1 **large leek, cut into ½-inch pieces**
1 **cup water**
¼ **teaspoon salt**
3 **cups broccoli flowerets**
¼ **cup whipping cream**
⅓ **cup mayonnaise *or* salad dressing**
¼ **cup crumbled blue cheese (1 ounce)**
4 **large leaves Bibb *or* Boston lettuce**

In a large saucepan combine carrots, leek, water, and salt. Bring to boiling; reduce heat. Cover and simmer 4 minutes. Add broccoli; cover and simmer 4 minutes more or till vegetables are crisp-tender (see photo 3, page 50). Drain. Cover and chill 2 to 24 hours.

For dressing, beat whipping cream with an electric mixer on high speed till soft peaks form. Gently fold in mayonnaise or salad dressing and blue cheese.

Line 4 individual salad plates with Bibb or Boston lettuce (see photo 4, page 27). Arrange vegetables atop lettuce. Dollop each salad with dressing. (*Or*, pour dressing over chilled vegetables. Toss to coat. Spoon salad onto lettuce-lined salad plates.) Makes 4 servings.

Potato and Beet Salad

Our taste panel described this salad as being a pretty rose color (the color comes from the beets), with a scrumptious sweet and sour dressing.

3 **medium potatoes (1 pound)**
1 **small apple, cored (see photo 2, page 20)**
1 **8¼-ounce can diced beets, drained and rinsed, *or* ¾ cup diced cooked beets**
3 **tablespoons salad oil**
3 **tablespoons tarragon vinegar**
1 **teaspoon sugar**
¼ **teaspoon salt**
4 **leaves romaine *or* Boston lettuce**

In a saucepan cook potatoes, covered, in boiling lightly salted water about 20 minutes or till tender (see photo 1, page 50). Drain; cool potatoes slightly. Cut potatoes into bite-size pieces (see photo 2, page 50).

Meanwhile, cut apple into thin wedges. Cut wedges crosswise in half. In a mixing bowl combine potato pieces, apple, and beets.

In a screw-top jar combine salad oil, vinegar, sugar, and salt. Cover and shake well. Pour over potato mixture. Toss to coat. Cover and chill 2 to 24 hours. Before serving, spoon salad onto lettuce-lined salad plates. Makes 4 servings.

◄ *Pictured opposite: Blue Cheese Garden Salad*

Pasta Salads With Pizzazz

Lasagna with meat sauce . . . step aside. Pasta salads are here! Wagon wheels or bow ties, spaghetti or fettuccine, macaroni or tortellini, spaetzle or rosamarina— take your pick.

Cook each shapely pasta to perfection, then toss with your favorite fruits, vegetables, or greens. Top the salads off with dazzling salad dressings that tickle your taste buds.

Tortellini and Cucumber Salad

Tortellini and Cucumber Salad

1	6- *or* 7-ounce package frozen tortellini
¼	cup olive oil *or* salad oil
3	tablespoons white *or* rosé wine
2	tablespoons lemon juice
1	tablespoon snipped fresh basil, tarragon, *or* thyme; *or* 1 teaspoon dried basil, tarragon, *or* thyme, crushed
1	teaspoon honey
½	teaspoon salt
2	cups torn salad greens (see pages 8–9)
1	small cucumber, halved lengthwise and sliced
¾	cup crumbled feta cheese (3 ounces)
¼	cup pine nuts *or* slivered almonds, toasted

Cook tortellini in boiling lightly salted water about 10 minutes or till al dente (see photo 1). Drain. Rinse with cold water (see photo 2). Drain well.

For dressing, in a screw-top jar combine oil, wine, lemon juice, herb, honey, and salt. Cover and shake well; pour over tortellini (see photo 3). Cover and chill 2 to 24 hours (see photo 4).

In a large bowl combine pasta, torn greens, cucumber, feta cheese, and pine nuts. Toss to coat (see photo 5). Serve immediately. Serves 5 or 6.

2 After draining the pasta, rinse it under cold water for several minutes. Rinsing cools the pasta, stops the cooking process, and helps remove excess starch. After rinsing, drain thoroughly.

1 Use a fork to remove one tortellini; transfer it to a cutting board. Using the edge of the fork, cut into the tortellini. Or, bite into the tortellini. It should be tender, but still slightly firm. This is a stage the Italians call *al dente*, meaning "to the tooth."

3 Pour the dressing over the pasta. Stir or toss the pasta to distribute the dressing evenly.

4 Chilling the pasta and dressing together allows the pasta to completely cool while the dressing flavors the pasta. Stir the mixture occasionally during chilling to distribute the dressing.

5 Using two salad servers, toss the salad. Be sure to get to the bottom of the bowl to thoroughly combine the dressing and ingredients.

Asparagus and Pasta Salad

1 **8-ounce package frozen cut asparagus** *or* **¾ pound fresh asparagus, cut into 1-inch pieces**
3 **ounces fettuccine** *or* **spaghetti**
1 **large tomato, peeled, seeded, and chopped**
⅓ **cup sliced pitted ripe olives**
2 **tablespoons snipped parsley**
¼ **cup vinegar**
2 **tablespoons olive oil** *or* **salad oil**
1 **clove garlic, minced**
1 **teaspoon dried oregano, crushed**
½ **teaspoon dried basil, crushed**
¼ **cup crumbled feta cheese (1 ounce)**

Cook frozen asparagus according to package directions. (*Or,* cook fresh asparagus in a small amount of boiling salted water for 7 to 8 minutes.) Drain asparagus; set aside. Cook fettuccine or spaghetti in boiling lightly salted water about 10 minutes or till al dente (see photo 1, page 58). Drain. Rinse with cold water (see photo 2, page 58). Drain well.

In a bowl combine asparagus, fettuccine or spaghetti, tomato, olives, and parsley.

For dressing, in a screw-top jar combine vinegar, olive or salad oil, garlic, oregano, and basil. Cover and shake well. Pour dressing over pasta mixture (see photo 3, page 59). Toss to coat. Cover and chill 2 to 24 hours (see photo 4, page 59). Before serving, add feta cheese. Toss to coat (see photo 5, page 59). Makes 4 servings.

Shells and Cheeses Salad

A trio of cheeses—cheddar, cottage, and blue—headline this all-star salad.

4 **ounces tiny shell macaroni (about 1⅓ cups)**
1 **cup sliced celery**
1 **cup shredded cheddar cheese (4 ounces)**
½ **cup cottage cheese, drained**
¼ **cup sliced green onion**
¼ **cup crumbled blue cheese (1 ounce)**
2 **tablespoons snipped parsley**
¼ **cup salad oil**
2 **tablespoons lemon juice**
1 **tablespoon Dijon-style mustard**
½ **teaspoon sugar**

Cook macaroni in boiling lightly salted water about 10 minutes or till al dente (see photo 1, page 58). Drain. Rinse with cold water (see photo 2, page 58). Drain well.

In a large bowl combine macaroni, celery, cheddar cheese, cottage cheese, green onion, blue cheese, and parsley.

For dressing, in a screw-top jar combine salad oil, lemon juice, mustard, and sugar. Cover and shake well. Pour dressing over pasta mixture (see photo 3, page 59). Toss to coat. Cover and chill 2 to 24 hours (see photo 4, page 59). Before serving, toss salad (see photo 5, page 59). Makes 4 servings.

Cavatelli-Artichoke Salad

Fines herbes (feen ZEHRB) is an aromatic combination of chives, tarragon, and chervil.

3 ounces cavatelli *or* tiny shell macaroni (about 2 cups)
1 14-ounce can artichoke hearts, drained and quartered
1 4-ounce can sliced *or* whole small mushrooms, drained
¾ cup thinly sliced celery
¼ cup sliced green onion
¼ cup sliced radishes
¼ cup snipped parsley
¼ cup olive oil *or* salad oil
2 tablespoons tarragon vinegar
1 teaspoon dried fines herbes, crushed
½ teaspoon sugar
¼ teaspoon salt
2 cups finely shredded lettuce

Cook cavatelli or tiny shell macaroni in boiling lightly salted water about 10 minutes or till al dente (see photo 1, page 58). Drain. Rinse with cold water (see photo 2, page 58). Drain well.

In a large bowl combine cavatelli or macaroni, artichoke hearts, mushrooms, celery, green onion, radishes, and snipped parsley.

For dressing, in a screw-top jar combine oil, vinegar, fines herbes, sugar, and salt. Cover and shake well. Pour dressing over pasta mixture (see photo 3, page 59). Toss to coat. Cover and chill 2 to 24 hours (see photo 4, page 59).

Using a slotted spoon, transfer salad to lettuce-lined serving platter or individual salad plates. Makes 4 servings.

Creamy Macaroni-Fruit Salad

2½ ounces elbow macaroni (about ¾ cup)
1 beaten egg
⅓ cup unsweetened pineapple juice
2 tablespoons sugar
1 tablespoon lemon juice
⅓ cup whipping cream
⅓ cup coarsely chopped pecans *or* walnuts
1 11-ounce can pineapple tidbits and mandarin orange sections, drained and chilled
1 medium apple, cored and chopped (see photo 2, page 20)
Lettuce leaves

Cook elbow macaroni in boiling lightly salted water for 8 to 10 minutes or till al dente (see photo 1, page 58). Drain. Rinse with cold water (see photo 2, page 58). Drain well.

For dressing, in a small saucepan combine beaten egg, pineapple juice, sugar, and lemon juice. Cook and stir over medium heat till thickened and bubbly, then cook and stir 1 minute more. Pour dressing over macaroni (see photo 3, page 59). Toss to coat. Cover and chill 2 to 24 hours (see photo 4, page 59).

Before serving, beat whipping cream with an electric mixer on high speed till soft peaks form. Reserve *1 tablespoon* pecans or walnuts; set aside. Fold whipped cream, remaining pecans or walnuts, pineapple tidbits and mandarin orange sections, and apple into pasta mixture.

Spoon salad onto lettuce-lined salad plates. Sprinkle with reserved nuts. Makes 6 servings.

Fruity Pasta Salad

1 slightly beaten egg
⅓ cup orange juice
3 tablespoons honey
2 tablespoons lemon juice
⅛ teaspoon ground cardamom
3 ounces bow ties *or* wagon wheels
    (about 1¾ cups)
1 cup sliced fresh peaches, orange
    sections, *or* melon cubes *or* balls
½ cup sliced celery
1 cup torn salad greens (see pages 8–9)
½ cup sliced strawberries

For dressing, in a small saucepan combine egg, orange juice, honey, lemon juice, and cardamom. Cook and stir over medium heat till thickened and bubbly. Cool slightly. Cover and chill.

Cook bow ties or wagon wheels in boiling lightly salted water for 12 to 15 minutes or till al dente (see photo 1, page 58). Drain. Rinse with cold water (see photo 2, page 58). Drain well.

In a large bowl combine bow ties, 1 cup assorted fruit, and celery. Pour dressing over pasta mixture (see photo 3, page 59). Toss to coat. Cover and chill 2 to 24 hours (see photo 4, page 59). Before serving, add salad greens and strawberries. Toss to coat (see photo 5, page 59). Makes 6 servings.

Shrimp and Spaetzle Salad

Spaetzle (SHPETS luh) is a favorite central European egg pasta. These tiny pasta pieces are dumpling-like in texture and taste.

½ of a 10½-ounce package spaetzle (1 cup)
2 4½-ounce cans large shrimp, rinsed and
    drained
1 large tomato, peeled, seeded, and
    coarsely chopped
2 tablespoons sliced green onion
⅓ cup mayonnaise *or* salad dressing
2 tablespoons lemon juice
1 tablespoon honey
¼ teaspoon ground ginger
2 cups chopped spinach

Cook spaetzle in boiling lightly salted water for 10 minutes. Remove from heat. Let stand, covered, for 10 minutes. Drain. Rinse with cold water (see photo 2, page 58). Drain well.

In a large bowl combine spaetzle, shrimp, tomato, and green onion.

For dressing, in a small bowl combine mayonnaise or salad dressing, lemon juice, honey, and ginger. Pour dressing over pasta mixture (see photo 3, page 59). Toss to coat. Cover and chill 2 to 24 hours (see photo 4, page 59). Before serving, add chopped spinach. Toss to coat (see photo 5, page 59). Makes 4 main-dish servings.

◀ *Pictured opposite: Fruity Pasta Salad*

Refreshing Rice Salads

Once you've mastered the technique of cooking rice, you'll want to put your skills to use. Why not sample Fruity Rice Salad, featuring long grain rice and an enchanting curry flavor? Or, try Ham and Lima Salad with chewy brown rice, bits of ham, and tender lima beans smothered in a creamy cucumber dressing.

Want more? Then turn the page for a look at recipes that help rice go beyond a hot side dish.

Oriental Rice Salad

Oriental Rice Salad

⅓ cup wild rice
1¾ cups water
⅛ teaspoon salt
⅓ cup long grain rice
2 tablespoons salad oil
2 tablespoons rice wine vinegar *or* vinegar
2 teaspoons soy sauce
2 teaspoons honey
¼ teaspoon ground ginger
¼ cup slivered almonds
1 6-ounce package frozen pea pods

Rinse wild rice under cold water about 1 minute (see photo 1). In a small saucepan bring wild rice, water, and salt to boiling (see photo 2). Reduce heat. Cover and simmer 30 minutes. Stir in long grain rice (see photo 3). Return to boiling; reduce heat. Cover and simmer 15 to 20 minutes more or till water is absorbed and rice is done (see photo 4). Remove from heat. Let stand, covered, for 10 minutes.

For dressing, in a small screw-top jar combine salad oil, vinegar, soy sauce, honey, and ginger. Cover and shake well. Transfer rice to a mixing bowl. Pour dressing over rice mixture. Toss to coat. Cover and chill 3 to 24 hours. Toast slivered almonds (see photo 5). Store in a covered container.

Before serving, place pea pods in a colander. Rinse pea pods under warm water to thaw. Add pea pods and toasted almonds to salad; toss to coat. Makes 6 servings.

1 Place wild rice in a strainer. (Make sure the strainer has small holes so the rice doesn't fall through.) Rinse the wild rice under cold water about 1 minute, lifting it with your fingers to rinse thoroughly. Rinsing the rice removes any dirt.

3 Stir in the long grain rice 30 minutes after the wild rice has started cooking. Long grain rice cooks faster than wild rice, so give wild rice a head start and they'll be done at the same time.

2 Bring the wild rice, water, and salt to boiling over high heat. Reduce the heat and cover. This allows the rice to simmer slowly.

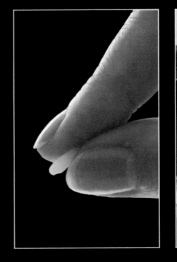

4 Test the long grain rice for doneness by pinching a grain (or a few grains) between your thumb and forefinger. If there is a hard core, cook the rice a little longer. Wild rice can't be tested this way, so cook it according to our timings.

5 To toast almonds, place them in a small skillet. Cook over medium heat, stirring constantly for even browning. The nuts will be golden brown in about 5 to 7 minutes. Remove them from the heat immediately.

Ham and Lima Salad

You'll find the cooking time for brown rice is longer than that of long grain rice. Its chewy texture and nut-like flavor make it worth those extra minutes.

1½   **cups water**
⅔   **cup brown rice**
⅛   **teaspoon salt**
½   **of an 8-ounce package frozen baby lima beans**
1½   **cups cubed fully cooked ham (8 ounces)**
1   **small green pepper, coarsely chopped**
¼   **cup thinly sliced green onion**
¼   **cup sliced pitted ripe olives**
2   **tablespoons snipped parsley**
1   **cup bottled creamy cucumber salad dressing**
     Lettuce cups *or* lettuce leaves (optional)
2   **hard-cooked eggs, sliced**

In a small saucepan bring water, rice, and salt to boiling (see photo 2, page 67). Reduce heat. Cover and simmer 40 to 50 minutes or till water is absorbed and rice is done (see photo 4, page 67). Remove from heat. Let stand, covered, for 10 minutes. Cook lima beans according to package directions; drain.

In a bowl combine rice, lima beans, ham, green pepper, green onion, olives, and parsley. Pour cucumber salad dressing over rice mixture. Toss to coat. Cover and chill 3 to 24 hours.

Before serving, spoon salad into lettuce cups or onto lettuce-lined plates, if desired. Top with egg slices. Makes 4 main-dish servings.

Mushroom-and-Bacon Rice Salad

¼   **cup wild rice***
1¼   **cups water**
⅛   **teaspoon salt**
¼   **cup long grain rice***
1½   **cups sliced fresh mushrooms**
1   **medium tomato, peeled, seeded, and coarsely chopped**
3   **slices bacon, crisp-cooked, drained, and crumbled**
2   **tablespoons sliced green onion**
3   **tablespoons salad oil**
3   **tablespoons lemon juice**
1   **teaspoon dried dillweed**
¼   **teaspoon garlic salt**
     Spinach *or* lettuce leaves

Rinse wild rice under cold water about 1 minute (see photo 1, page 66). In a small saucepan bring wild rice, water, and salt to boiling (see photo 2, page 67). Reduce heat. Cover and simmer 30 minutes. Stir in long grain rice (see photo 3, page 67). Return to boiling; reduce heat. Cover and simmer 15 to 20 minutes more or till water is absorbed and rice is done (see photo 4, page 67). Remove from heat. Let stand, covered, for 10 minutes.

In a medium mixing bowl combine rice, mushrooms, tomato, bacon, and green onion.

For dressing, in a small screw-top jar combine salad oil, lemon juice, dillweed, and garlic salt. Cover and shake well. Pour dressing over rice mixture. Toss to coat. Cover and chill 3 to 24 hours. Serve on spinach- or lettuce-lined plates. If desired, garnish with additional tomato. Makes 6 servings.

***Note:** If desired, substitute ½ cup *brown rice* for the ¼ cup wild rice and ¼ cup long grain rice. Cook brown rice 40 to 50 minutes, covered, or till water is absorbed and rice is done. Continue as directed.

Creamy Chicken-and-Rice Salad

1 cup water
½ cup long grain rice
1 teaspoon instant chicken bouillon granules
1½ cups cubed cooked chicken (8 ounces)
2 medium tomatoes, peeled, seeded, and chopped
½ cup chopped celery *or* peeled, diced jicama
½ cup frozen peas
1 8-ounce carton dairy sour cream
3 tablespoons dry white wine
½ teaspoon salt
½ teaspoon dried tarragon, crushed
⅛ teaspoon pepper
4 lettuce cups
Parsley sprigs (optional)

In a small saucepan bring water, rice, and chicken bouillon granules to boiling (see photo 2, page 67). Reduce heat. Cover and simmer 15 to 20 minutes or till water is absorbed and rice is done (see photo 4, page 67). Remove from heat. Let stand, covered, for 10 minutes.

In a medium mixing bowl combine rice, chicken, tomatoes, celery or jicama, and peas.

For dressing, in a small mixing bowl combine sour cream, wine, salt, tarragon, and pepper. Pour dressing over rice mixture. Toss to coat. Cover and chill 3 to 24 hours. If necessary, add milk to moisten. Before serving, spoon salad into lettuce cups. Garnish with parsley, if desired. Makes 4 main-dish servings.

Fruit and Rice Salad

Go tropical! For another sensational flavor combination, substitute a can of drained pineapple chunks for the mandarin orange sections.

1⅓ cups water
⅔ cup long grain rice*
⅛ teaspoon salt
1 11-ounce can mandarin orange sections, drained
1 small apple, cored and chopped (see photo 2, page 20)
½ cup seedless red *or* green grapes, halved
¼ cup raisins
½ cup plain yogurt
¼ cup mayonnaise *or* salad dressing
1 tablespoon chopped chutney
1 to 2 teaspoons curry powder
⅛ teaspoon salt
⅛ teaspoon pepper
½ cup coarsely chopped peanuts
Romaine *or* leaf lettuce

In a saucepan bring water, rice, and ⅛ teaspoon salt to boiling (see photo 2, page 67). Reduce heat. Cover and simmer 15 to 20 minutes or till water is absorbed and rice is done (see photo 4, page 67). Remove from heat. Let stand, covered, for 10 minutes.

In a mixing bowl combine rice, mandarin oranges, apple, grapes, and raisins.

For dressing, in a small mixing bowl stir together yogurt, mayonnaise or salad dressing, chutney, curry, ⅛ teaspoon salt, and pepper. Pour dressing over rice mixture. Toss to coat. Cover and chill 3 to 24 hours.

If necessary, add milk to moisten. Before serving, stir in peanuts. Serve in lettuce-lined bowl or on lettuce-lined salad plates. Serves 8.

---

*Note: If desired, substitute ⅔ cup *brown rice* for the ⅔ cup long grain rice. Prepare as directed, *except* use 1½ cups water. Cook brown rice 40 to 50 minutes, covered, or till water is absorbed and rice is tender. Continue as directed.

Gelatin Gems

These yummy salads all start with packaged flavored gelatin. To this easy beginning add chunks of fresh fruit, bits of chopped nuts, or smooth, creamy yogurt.

The results: Salads in every color of the rainbow. Sample some of these shimmering beauties, and find that each wiggle and jiggle explodes with flavor.

Strawberry and Apple Salad

Strawberry and Apple Salad

If you don't want to make shaky shapes from the gelatin, pour the mixture into a 9x5x3-inch pan. Chill, then cut into squares.

1¼ **cups apple juice *or* cider**
1 **4-serving-size package strawberry-flavored gelatin**
1 **tablespoon lemon juice**
1 **cup applesauce**

In a saucepan heat *¾ cup* apple juice to boiling; remove from heat. Add strawberry-flavored gelatin; stir till dissolved (see photo 1). Stir in remaining apple juice and lemon juice (see photo 2). Chill till partially set (see photo 3).

Stir in applesauce (see photo 4). Line a 9x9x2-inch pan or dish with clear plastic wrap. Leave enough plastic wrap to hang over the edge of the pan. Pour gelatin mixture into the pan. Chill at least 6 hours or till firm. Before serving, cut gelatin into shapes (see photo 5). Transfer to lettuce-lined salad plates; garnish with apple slices and decorate with mayonnaise and raisins, if desired. Serves 4 to 6.

1 Add the flavored gelatin to the hot liquid. Stir with a spoon to dissolve the gelatin. Scrape the sides and bottom of the saucepan well to make sure all of the gelatin granules are completely dissolved.

2 Stir the remaining apple juice into the gelatin mixture. The second addition of liquid should be cold or at room temperature. This liquid cools the gelatin mixture and starts the thickening process.

3 Place gelatin in the refrigerator till partially set. At this stage, the consistency is similar to unbeaten egg whites. Or, quick-chill gelatin by placing the saucepan in a large bowl of ice water; stir occasionally.

4 Stir the applesauce into the partially set gelatin. Partially setting the gelatin before adding the fruit helps keep the fruit distributed so it won't settle in the bottom or float to the top of the salad.

5 Carefully lift the clear plastic wrap and gelatin from the pan to a hard, flat surface. Use cookie cutters to cut the gelatin into shapes, placing the cookie cutters as close together as possible. Cut through to the bottom of the gelatin. Remove shapes with a spatula.

Lime and Grape Salad

1 **cup water**
1 **4-serving-size package lime-flavored gelatin**
1 **cup white grape juice**
1 **medium banana, peeled and thinly sliced**
½ **cup seedless red *or* green grapes, halved**
   Lettuce leaves (optional)

In a saucepan heat water to boiling; remove from heat. Add lime-flavored gelatin; stir till dissolved (see photo 1, page 72). Stir in white grape juice (see photo 2, page 72). Chill till partially set (see photo 3, page 73).

Stir in banana and grapes (see photo 4, page 73). Pour into a 9x5x3-inch pan or six 6-ounce custard cups. Chill for at least 6 hours or till firm. If using a 9x5x3-inch pan, loosen edges of salad with a knife, then cut into 6 pieces. Serve on lettuce-lined plates, if desired. Serves 6.

Very Berry Puff

Transform this salad into a delightful dessert—just dollop each serving with frozen whipped dessert topping and sprinkle with toasted almonds.

1 **cup water**
1 **4-serving-size package raspberry- *or* strawberry-flavored gelatin**
1 **8-ounce carton raspberry *or* strawberry yogurt**

In a saucepan heat water to boiling; remove from heat. Add raspberry- *or* strawberry-flavored gelatin; stir till dissolved (see photo 1, page 72).

Add yogurt. Transfer mixture to a small mixer bowl. Beat with an electric mixer on low speed till combined. Chill till partially set (see photo 3, page 73).

Beat with an electric mixer on high speed till doubled in volume. Pour mixture into an 8x8x2-inch pan or six 6-ounce custard cups. Chill at least 6 hours or till firm. If using an 8x8x2-inch pan, loosen edges of salad with a knife, then cut into 6 pieces. Makes 6 servings.

Cranberry-Orange Salad

A double dose of orange and cranberry gives the salad a tangy, festive flavor.

1 **cup cranberry juice cocktail**
1 **4-serving-size package orange-flavored gelatin**
½ **cup cranberry juice cocktail**
1 **10-ounce package frozen cranberry-orange relish, thawed**
   Lettuce leaves
   Frozen whipped dessert topping, thawed
   Orange slices (optional)

In a saucepan heat 1 cup cranberry juice cocktail to boiling; remove from heat. Add orange-flavored gelatin; stir till dissolved (see photo 1, page 72). Stir in ½ cup cranberry juice cocktail (see photo 2, page 72). Chill till partially set (see photo 3, page 73).

Fold in cranberry-orange relish (see photo 4, page 73). Pour into an 8x4x2-inch pan. Chill at least 6 hours or till firm. Before serving, loosen the edges of the salad with a knife, then cut into 6 pieces. Place on lettuce-lined salad plates. Dollop with dessert topping. Garnish with orange slices, if desired. Makes 6 servings.

Golden Salad

Paper-thin pieces of bark from the cinnamon tree are used to make what we know as stick cinnamon. Stick cinnamon and whole cloves in this recipe give the salad a delicate spice flavor without clouding the gelatin.

1 cup unsweetened pineapple *or* orange juice
¼ cup light raisins
2 3-inch pieces stick cinnamon
4 whole cloves
1 4-serving-size package orange-pineapple-flavored gelatin
1 cup ginger ale
1 11-ounce can pineapple tidbits and mandarin orange sections, drained

---

In a small saucepan combine pineapple or orange juice, raisins, stick cinnamon, and cloves. Bring to boiling; cover. Reduce heat; simmer for 5 minutes. Remove from heat. Remove spices.

Add orange-pineapple-flavored gelatin; stir till dissolved (see photo 1, page 72). Stir in ginger ale (see photo 2, page 72). Chill till partially set (see photo 3, page 73).

Stir in pineapple and orange sections (see photo 4, page 73). Pour into an 8x8x2-inch pan or a 1-quart serving bowl. Chill at least 6 hours or till firm. If using an 8x8x2-inch pan loosen the edges of the salad with a knife, then cut into squares. Makes 4 to 6 servings.

Snappy Tomato Cubes

1 10-ounce can hot-style vegetable juice cocktail
2 tablespoons lemon juice
½ teaspoon Worcestershire sauce
Few dashes bottled hot pepper sauce
Dash garlic powder
1 4-serving-size package lemon-flavored gelatin
⅓ cup cold water
4 lettuce *or* romaine leaves
¼ cup dairy sour cream *or* plain yogurt
2 tablespoons milk
1 tablespoon chopped green pepper *or* green onion

In a saucepan combine vegetable juice cocktail, lemon juice, Worcestershire sauce, hot pepper sauce, and garlic powder. Bring to boiling; remove from heat. Add lemon-flavored gelatin; stir till dissolved (see photo 1, page 72). Stir in cold water (see photo 2, page 72). Pour into a 9x5x3-inch pan. Chill at least 6 hours or till firm.

Before serving, loosen edges of salad with a knife, then cut into ½-inch cubes. Arrange cubes on lettuce-lined salad plates.

In a small mixing bowl combine sour cream and milk. (*Or,* if using yogurt, omit milk.) Drizzle over salads. Sprinkle with chopped green pepper or green onion. Makes 4 servings.

Molded Gelatin Salads

Add flair to your next meal with one of these glittering gelatin salads.

Cool and refreshing, these tasty salads complement any lunch or dinner. Each salad stands on its own—no salad dressings needed here to add flavor! Just unmold and you're ready to enjoy.

Layered Vegetable Aspic

Layered Vegetable Aspic

Salad oil
2   14½-ounce cans chicken broth
2   envelopes unflavored gelatin
1   teaspoon finely shredded lemon peel
2   tablespoons sugar
2   tablespoons dry sherry
1½ cups finely shredded cabbage
½   cup shredded carrot
1   tablespoon finely chopped green onion
½   teaspoon dried dillweed
1   whole green onion
1   cup frozen loose-pack baby peas

Lightly oil a 2-quart soufflé dish. In a saucepan combine *1 can* broth, gelatin, and peel. Let stand 5 minutes (see photo 1). Cook and stir over medium heat till gelatin is dissolved. Stir in remaining broth, sugar, and sherry. Pour ¼ *cup* gelatin into soufflé dish. Chill till almost firm.

Meanwhile, in a bowl combine cabbage, carrot, chopped onion, and dillweed; set aside. Cook whole green onion in boiling water 30 seconds or till limp. Place onion on gelatin layer in soufflé dish, fanning out top of onion. Arrange peas over gelatin layer (see photo 2). Pour ½ *cup* of gelatin over peas; chill till almost firm.

Meanwhile, chill remaining gelatin till partially set (see photo 3). Stir cabbage mixture into partially set gelatin (see photo 4, page 73). Carefully spoon cabbage mixture over pea layer (see photo 4). Chill at least 6 hours or till firm. Unmold salad onto a serving plate (see photo 5). If desired, garnish with lemon slices, mayonnaise or salad dressing, and parsley. Serves 6 to 8.

1 Sprinkle gelatin over the chicken broth, as shown. Let stand for 5 minutes. This process is known as softening. During this time the gelatin granules soften in the liquid so dissolving the gelatin is easier.

2 Arrange peas evenly on the gelatin layer. The gelatin should be *almost* firm (sticky when touched). If the gelatin is not almost firm, the peas will sink. If the gelatin is too firm, the peas will not adhere to the gelatin.

3 To quickly start the gelling process, place the saucepan in a bowl of ice and water. Using a spoon, stir the gelatin mixture as it sets up.

4 Spoon the cabbage mixture over the almost-firm pea layer. If the pea layer is not firm enough, the cabbage layer will mix with the pea layer. But, if the gelatin has set too long, the two layers will not adhere to each other.

5 Dip the mold in warm water for a few seconds. Then, run a knife around the edge. Center a plate upside-down over the mold. Holding the mold and plate together, invert them. Shake the mold gently and carefully lift it off. If the salad doesn't unmold, repeat the procedure.

Burgundy-Grape Mold

Salad oil
1   **cup water**
1   **6-ounce can frozen cranberry juice concentrate, thawed**
¼   **cup Burgundy**
1   **tablespoon honey**
1   **envelope unflavored gelatin**
1   **3-ounce package cream cheese, cut up**
¼   **teaspoon finely shredded orange peel**
1   **orange, peeled, sectioned, and cut-up (see photo 1, page 20)**
½   **cup seedless red *or* green grapes, halved**
    Leaf lettuce (optional)

Lightly oil a 3-cup mold; set aside. In a saucepan combine water, cranberry juice concentrate, Burgundy, honey, and gelatin. Let stand 5 minutes to soften (see photo 1, page 78). Cook and stir over medium heat till gelatin is dissolved. Pour ¾ *cup* of the gelatin mixture into the mold. Chill till almost firm.

Meanwhile, pour the remaining gelatin mixture into a blender or food processor container. Add cream cheese and orange peel. Cover; blend or process till smooth. Chill till partially set (see photo 3, page 73).

Stir orange pieces and grapes into partially set gelatin (see photo 4, page 73). Carefully spoon over gelatin layer in mold (see photo 4, page 79). Chill at least 6 hours or till firm.

Dip mold in warm water a few seconds to loosen edges. Unmold salad onto a serving plate (see photo 5, page 79). Garnish with leaf lettuce, if desired. Makes 4 to 6 servings.

Apple-Raisin Salad

These individual fruity salads are perfect anytime you're looking for a light, refreshing salad.

Salad oil
1   **cup apple juice**
¼   **cup raisins *or* currants, chopped**
1   **4-serving-size package lemon- *or* orange-flavored gelatin**
¾   **cup cold water**
1   **small apple, cored and finely chopped (see photo 2, page 20)**
    Leaf lettuce *or* spinach leaves (optional)

Lightly oil four ½-cup molds; set aside. In a saucepan combine apple juice and raisins or currants. Bring to boiling; remove from heat. Add lemon- or orange-flavored gelatin; stir till dissolved (see photo 1, page 72). Stir in cold water (see photo 2, page 72). Chill till partially set (see photo 3, page 73).

Stir apple into partially set gelatin (see photo 4, page 73). Evenly divide gelatin mixture among the molds. Chill at least 3 hours or till firm.

Dip molds in warm water for a few seconds to loosen edges. Unmold salads onto individual salad plates (see photo 5, page 79). Garnish with leaf lettuce or spinach leaves, if desired. Makes 4 servings.

Zippy Gazpacho Molds

Presto, chango! We turned gazpacho, a cold soup made with tomatoes, green pepper, and cucumber, into a tantalizing salad.

   Salad oil
¼ cup water
1 envelope unflavored gelatin
1 tablespoon lemon juice
¼ teaspoon onion powder
1 12-ounce can vegetable juice cocktail
½ cup seeded and chopped cucumber
2 tablespoons chopped green pepper
   Lettuce (optional)
   Dairy sour cream *or* mayonnaise
     (optional)

Lightly oil four ½-cup molds; set aside. In a saucepan combine water, gelatin, lemon juice, and onion powder. Let stand 5 minutes to soften (see photo 1, page 78). Cook and stir over medium heat till gelatin is dissolved. Add vegetable juice cocktail. Chill till partially set (see photo 3, page 73).

Stir cucumber and green pepper into partially set gelatin (see photo 4, page 73). Evenly divide the gelatin mixture among the molds. Chill at least 3 hours or till firm.

Dip molds in warm water for a few seconds to loosen edges. Unmold onto individual plates (see photo 5, page 79). Garnish with lettuce and dollop with sour cream or mayonnaise, if desired. Makes 4 servings.

Rum Fruit Molds

   Salad oil
½ cup mixed dried fruit bits
½ cup water
3 tablespoons light rum
1 4-serving-size package apricot- *or*
     orange-pineapple-flavored gelatin
1 cup cold water
¼ cup chopped pecans
   Leaf lettuce (optional)

Lightly oil six ½-cup molds; set aside. In a saucepan combine fruit bits, ½ cup water, and rum. Bring to boiling; reduce heat. Cover, then cook for 5 minutes; do not drain.

Add apricot- or orange-pineapple-flavored gelatin to fruit mixture; stir till dissolved (see photo 1, page 72). Stir in 1 cup cold water (see photo 2, page 72). Chill till partially set (see photo 3, page 73).

Stir pecans into partially set gelatin (see photo 4, page 73). Pour gelatin into molds. Chill at least 3 hours or till firm.

Dip molds in warm water for a few seconds to loosen edges. Unmold onto individual salad plates (see photo 5, page 79). Garnish with leaf lettuce, if desired. Makes 6 servings.

Summertime Melon-Lime Mold

You can skip the softening step here. Just combine the sugar and gelatin.

Salad oil
½ cup sugar
½ cup water
1 envelope unflavored gelatin
1 envelope *unsweetened* lemon-lime-flavored soft drink mix
1 10-ounce bottle ginger ale
1½ cups small honeydew melon balls
Vanilla yogurt (optional)

Lightly oil a 4-cup ring mold; set aside. In a medium saucepan combine sugar, water, gelatin, and soft drink mix. Cook and stir over medium heat till gelatin is dissolved, then remove from heat. Slowly add ginger ale. Let stand 10 minutes, stirring occasionally. Skim off foam. Chill till partially set (see photo 3, page 73).

Stir melon balls into partially set gelatin (see photo 4, page 73). Pour gelatin mixture into the mold. Chill at least 6 hours or till firm.

Dip mold in warm water for a few seconds to loosen edges. Unmold salad onto a serving plate (see photo 5, page 79). Dollop with yogurt, if desired. Makes 4 to 6 servings.

Summertime Melon-Orange Mold: Prepare Summertime Melon-Lime Mold as above, *except* substitute 1 envelope *unsweetened orange-flavored soft drink mix* and 1½ cups small *cantaloupe balls* for the lemon-lime-flavored soft drink mix and honeydew melon balls.

Cranberry-Nog Mold

Salad oil
¾ cup cranberry juice cocktail
1 4-serving-size package raspberry-flavored gelatin
1 14-ounce jar cranberry-orange sauce
¼ cup water
3½ teaspoons unflavored gelatin
1 tablespoon lemon juice
2 cups dairy *or* canned eggnog
¾ cup lemon *or* pineapple sherbet, softened
Frosted cranberries* (optional)
Mint leaves (optional)

Lightly oil a 5½-cup ring mold; set aside. In a saucepan heat cranberry juice to boiling, then remove from heat. Add raspberry-flavored gelatin; stir till dissolved (see photo 1, page 72). Stir in cranberry-orange sauce. Pour cranberry mixture into mold. Chill till almost firm (see photo 3, page 73).

In a saucepan combine water, unflavored gelatin, and lemon juice. Let stand 5 minutes to soften (see photo 1, page 78). Cook and stir over medium heat till gelatin is dissolved. Stir in eggnog and sherbet. Chill till partially set.

Carefully spoon eggnog layer over the cranberry mixture (see photo 4, page 79). Chill at least 6 hours or till firm.

Dip mold in warm water for a few seconds to loosen edges. Unmold salad onto a serving plate (see photo 5, page 79). If desired, garnish with frosted cranberries and mint leaves. Makes 8 to 10 servings.

***Note:** To frost cranberries, combine a slightly beaten *egg white* and a little *water*. Brush cranberries with egg white mixture. Sprinkle with sugar and place on rack to dry.

◄ *Pictured opposite: Cranberry-Nog Mold*

Wilted Salads

When you're hot you're hot—and these salads are definitely hot! A flash in the pan is all it takes to put together these wonderful wilted salads.

   Crisp bacon and its flavorful drippings form the base for a subtly seasoned dressing. These last-minute salads are done in minutes. Just toss in the greens and in only moments your salad wilts to perfection.

Wilted Romaine Salad

Wilted Romaine Salad

Green onion and orange add color and flavor to this year-round favorite.

 2 **slices bacon**
 2 **tablespoons white wine vinegar**
 ½ **teaspoon sugar**
 ⅛ **teaspoon dried basil, crushed**
 4 **cups torn romaine (see pages 8–9)**
 2 **tablespoons sliced green onion**
 1 **medium orange, peeled, sectioned, and cut up (see photo 1, page 20)**

Cut bacon into pieces (see photo 1). In a 12-inch skillet cook bacon till crisp (see photo 2). Stir vinegar, sugar, and crushed dried basil into bacon and bacon drippings; bring to boiling (see photo 3).

Add torn romaine and sliced green onion to dressing in the skillet. Toss for 30 to 60 seconds or till romaine is just wilted (see photo 4). Remove from heat. Add orange pieces; toss lightly. Transfer to a serving bowl. Serve immediately. Makes 4 servings.

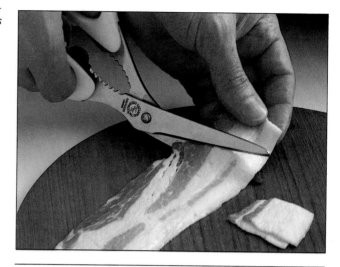

1 Using kitchen shears, snip the bacon into bite-size pieces. Or, if you don't have kitchen shears, use a sharp knife and a cutting board.

2 Place the bacon pieces in a large skillet; cook and stir over medium heat till the bacon is crisp and brown. Leave the cooked bacon and the drippings in the skillet.

Wilted Chinese Cabbage Salad

Chinese cabbage is a crisp, pale, crinkly-leaved green cabbage resembling romaine lettuce in shape and size.

3	cups torn Chinese cabbage (see pages 8–9)
3	cups torn spinach (see pages 8–9)
2	cups fresh bean sprouts *or* one 16-ounce can bean sprouts, drained
12	cherry tomatoes, halved
3	slices bacon
⅓	cup sliced green onion
2	tablespoons soy sauce
2	tablespoons water
2	tablespoons dry sherry
1	tablespoon honey
1	tablespoon lemon juice

In a large bowl combine Chinese cabbage, spinach, bean sprouts, and tomatoes. Set aside.

Cut bacon into pieces (see photo 1). In a 12-inch skillet cook bacon till crisp (see photo 2). Stir sliced green onion, soy sauce, water, sherry, honey, and lemon juice into bacon and bacon drippings; bring to boiling (see photo 3).

Add cabbage mixture to dressing in the skillet. Toss for 30 to 60 seconds or till greens are just wilted (see photo 4). Transfer to a serving bowl. Serve immediately. Makes 6 servings.

3 Add the vinegar, sugar, and basil to the skillet. Using a wooden spoon, stir the ingredients into the bacon drippings till combined. Heat the dressing mixture till bubbly.

4 Add torn romaine and onion to the the skillet. Using two spoons or forks, toss the romaine mixture to coat it evenly with the dressing. Cook and toss just till the romaine is *slightly* wilted, 30 to 60 seconds; do not overcook.

Edible Salad Bowls

You've seen round bowls, short ones, wide ones, wooden ones, and glass ones. But have you ever seen an edible salad bowl?

Each one of these scrumptious salad mixtures is tucked into its own edible container. Green peppers, papayas, zucchini, tortillas, or individual bread loaves double as the bowl. The only thing we left out is the fork!

Berry-Stuffed Papayas

Berry-Stuffed Papayas

To ripen papayas, let them stand at room temperature for 3 to 5 days or till the fruit yields to gentle pressure.

2   **large ripe papayas**
¼   **cup lemon yogurt**
1   **tablespoon honey**
½   **cup strawberries, hulled and sliced**
      (see photo 5, page 21)
½   **cup blueberries**
1   **large banana, sliced**
¼   **cup chopped pecans**

Peel and halve papayas lengthwise (see photo 1). Scoop out seeds; scoop out pulp, leaving a ½-inch-thick shell (see photo 2). Brush shells with *lemon juice*. Chop enough pulp to measure *½ cup* (see photo 3). Set aside. Reserve any remaining papaya pulp for another use.

In a mixing bowl stir together yogurt and honey. Stir in reserved ½ cup papaya, strawberries, blueberries, and banana (see photo 4). Spoon filling into 4 papaya shells (see photo 5). Sprinkle with pecans. Serve on a lettuce-lined platter, if desired. Makes 4 servings.

2 Using a spoon, scoop the seeds from the center of the fruit; discard seeds. After the seeds are removed, continue to scoop out the pulp of the papaya with the spoon to form a ½-inch-thick shell.

1 Hold the papaya firmly in one hand. Using a paring knife, remove the peel from the papaya, turning the papaya as you peel. Then cut the papaya lengthwise in half.

3 Place the papaya pulp on a cutting board and chop into bite-size pieces. Use any remaining papaya soon as a dessert or snack.

4 Gently stir the fruit into the yogurt-honey mixture. Be careful not to break up the fruit as you stir, yet make sure all the fruit is coated with the dressing.

5 Spoon filling into each shell. Mound the filling on top and around the edges of the papaya as necessary.

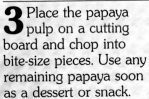

Confetti Salad In Pepper Shells

In minutes you'll be ready to enjoy this creamy salad.

3 **large green peppers**
1½ **cups cream-style cottage cheese,**
      drained
¼ **cup creamy cucumber salad dressing**
½ **cup shredded carrot (see photo 4,**
      page 15)
½ **cup finely chopped celery**
2 **tablespoons sliced green onion**

Halve green peppers lengthwise. Remove stems. Scoop out seeds and membranes (see photo 2, page 90).

In a mixing bowl stir together cottage cheese and cucumber dressing. Stir in carrot, celery, and onion (see photo 4, page 91). Spoon filling into pepper shells (see photo 5, page 91). Chill, if desired. Makes 6 servings.

Chicken Salad In Tortilla Bowls

1 **9-ounce package frozen artichoke hearts**
4 **8-inch flour tortillas**
3 **cups torn salad greens (see pages 8–9)**
2 **cups cubed cooked chicken (10 ounces)**
1 **medium sweet red *or* green pepper,**
      cut into 1-inch squares
½ **cup sliced fresh mushrooms**
⅓ **cup mayonnaise *or* salad dressing**
2 **tablespoons grated Parmesan cheese**
1 **tablespoon dry white wine**
⅛ **teaspoon dry mustard**

Cook artichoke hearts according to package directions; drain and chill. Meanwhile, brush *1* tortilla lightly with water to make it more pliable. Press tortilla into an ovenproof 10-ounce casserole. Repeat with remaining tortillas and 3 more casseroles. Place casseroles in a shallow baking pan. Bake in a 350° oven for 15 to 18 minutes or just till crisp. Cool. Remove from casseroles.

Halve or quarter any large artichoke hearts. In a large mixing bowl combine artichoke hearts, torn greens, chicken, red or green pepper, and mushrooms; gently toss. Spoon filling into tortilla shells (see photo 5, page 91).

For dressing, in a small mixing bowl combine mayonnaise or salad dressing, Parmesan cheese, wine, and mustard. Pass dressing with salads. Makes 4 main-dish servings.

Fruit-Filled Nectarines

1 **cup watermelon balls *or* chunks**
½ **cup sliced strawberries, raspberries,**
      ***or* blackberries**
¼ **cup sliced celery**
2 **tablespoons honey**
2 **tablespoons lime juice**
¼ **teaspoon poppy seed**
4 **large nectarines *or* peaches**
      Lime juice
      Lettuce leaves (optional)

In a medium mixing bowl combine watermelon, berries, and celery. For dressing, in a small bowl stir together honey, 2 tablespoons lime juice, and poppy seed. Pour dressing over fruit; toss to coat (see photo 4, page 91).

Halve nectarines or peaches; remove pit (see photo 4, page 21). If necessary, hollow out each nectarine or peach half, leaving a ½-inch-thick shell (see photo 2, page 90). Brush shells with additional lime juice. Spoon filling into the 8 shells (see photo 5, page 91). Serve on lettuce-lined plates, if desired. Makes 4 servings.

Mushroom-Avocado Stuffed Tomatoes

4   large tomatoes
⅓   cup mayonnaise *or* salad dressing
1   to 1½ teaspoons prepared horseradish
⅛   teaspoon salt
     Dash pepper
1   cup sliced fresh mushrooms
½   cup chopped celery
1   medium avocado
     Leaf lettuce (optional)
4   fluted mushrooms* (optional)

Cut a ½-inch slice from the stem end of each tomato. Scoop out tomato pulp, leaving a ½-inch-thick shell (see photo 2, page 90). Reserve pulp. Discard seeds and juices; chop remaining tomato pulp (see photo 3, page 91).

In a mixing bowl combine mayonnaise or salad dressing, horseradish, salt, and pepper. Stir in tomato pulp, sliced mushrooms, and celery. Halve, seed, and peel avocado. Cut avocado into bite-size pieces. Stir avocado into filling mixture (see photo 4, page 91). Spoon filling into tomato cups (see photo 5, page 91).

If desired, arrange stuffed tomatoes on lettuce-lined salad plates. Garnish each with a fluted mushroom, if desired. Serve tomatoes immediately. Makes 4 servings.

*Note: To make fluted mushrooms, hold a small sharp paring knife at an angle. Begin at the tip of the mushroom cap and carve a thin strip out of the cap in the form of an inverted "V." Turn the mushroom and continue cutting out inverted "V" strips in a spiral fashion, cutting out a total of 5 or 6 strips.

Salmon Salad in Bread Bowls

Save the bread you scoop out from the center of the loaves to use in a favorite meat loaf or stuffing recipe.

1   16-ounce loaf frozen whole wheat bread dough, thawed
1   15½-ounce can salmon
¼   cup mayonnaise *or* salad dressing
1   tablespoon Dijon-style mustard
¼   teaspoon dried dillweed
1   small cucumber, seeded and chopped (1 cup)
1   hard-cooked egg, peeled and chopped
2   tablespoons thinly sliced green onion
1   cup alfalfa sprouts
1   small tomato, seeded and chopped (optional)

Divide dough into 4 portions. Shape each portion into a small round loaf, 2¾ inches in diameter. Place loaves on a greased baking sheet. Cover and let rise for 35 to 45 minutes. Bake in a 350° oven for 20 to 25 minutes or till golden brown. Cool on a wire rack.

Meanwhile, drain salmon. Remove skin and bones; discard (see photo 1, page 26). Set salmon aside. In a mixing bowl stir together mayonnaise or salad dressing, mustard, and dillweed. Stir in cucumber, egg, and onion (see photo 4, page 91). Gently fold in salmon. Cover; chill.

Before serving, cut a slice off of the top of each bread loaf. Hollow out bread loaves, leaving a ¼- to ½-inch-thick bowl (see photo 2, page 90). Line each bread bowl with ¼ cup alfalfa sprouts. Spoon filling into bread bowls (see photo 5, page 91). Sprinkle with chopped tomato, if desired. Serve immediately. Makes 4 main-dish servings.

Dazzling Main-Dish Salads

What makes a main-dish salad really dazzle? In this case, it's the dressing. Start with creamy, homemade mayonnaise. From this modest beginning we show you how to make a variety of delectable dressings.

Underneath each dressing you'll find a hearty salad filled with fresh greens, crisp vegetables, and meats. Any one of these suppertime salads will fill you up and keep you going.

Seafood Salad

Creamy Mayonnaise

The flavor of this homemade mayonnaise in sand-wiches and salads is well worth the effort.

1 large egg
1 tablespoon vinegar
½ teaspoon salt
¼ teaspoon dry mustard
⅛ teaspoon paprika
Dash ground red pepper
1 cup salad oil
1 tablespoon lemon juice

In a blender container combine egg, vinegar, salt, dry mustard, paprika, and ground red pepper. Cover and blend about 5 seconds.

With blender running at low speed, gradually add *½ cup* salad oil (see photo 1). As necessary, stop blender and use a rubber spatula to scrape sides. Add lemon juice. With blender running at low speed, slowly add the remaining ½ cup salad oil till mayonnaise is thick and smooth (see photo 2).

To store, transfer mayonnaise to a tightly covered jar. Store up to 4 weeks in the refrigerator. Makes about 1¼ cups.

Note: You can make Creamy Mayonnaise in your food processor. Prepare recipe as directed above, *except* double the ingredients.

1 With the blender running, gradually add the salad oil in a thin, steady stream, as shown. If the lid does not have a hole in the center, lift the edge of the lid slightly and pour the oil slowly into the container. The oil must be added slowly to ensure a uniform, creamy emulsion.

2 The finished mayonnaise should be thick and smooth, as shown. If the mayonnaise does not form an emulsion, it will appear thin or curdled and will separate (see tip box, page 98).

Seafood Salad

If you're a real seafood lover, use half shrimp and half crab meat in this salad.

- ⅓ **cup Creamy Mayonnaise (see recipe, left)**
- 2 **tablespoons chili sauce**
- 2 **tablespoons finely chopped green onion**
- 1 **tablespoon snipped parsley**
- ½ **teaspoon lemon juice**
- **Several dashes bottled hot pepper sauce**
- ¼ **cup whipping cream**
- 5 **cups torn salad greens (see pages 8–9)**
- 12 **ounces frozen cooked shrimp** *or* **crab meat, thawed**
- 1 **medium avocado** **Lemon juice**
- 2 **medium tomatoes, cut into wedges**
- 2 **hard-cooked eggs, cut into wedges** **Paprika (optional)**

Prepare Creamy Mayonnaise (see photos 1–2, page 96). For dressing, in a mixing bowl combine ⅓ cup Creamy Mayonnaise, chili sauce, green onion, parsley, lemon juice, and hot pepper sauce. In a small mixer bowl beat whipping cream with an electric mixer on high speed till soft peaks form. Fold whipped cream into mayonnaise mixture (see photo 1). Cover and chill.

Evenly divide torn salad greens among 4 individual salad plates. Arrange shrimp or crab on torn greens.

Halve, seed, peel, and slice avocado. Brush avocado slices with lemon juice. Arrange avocado slices, tomato wedges, and hard-cooked egg wedges around seafood (see photo 2). Sprinkle with paprika, if desired. Pass dressing with salads. Makes 4 main-dish servings.

1 Gently fold the whipped cream into the mayonnaise mixture with a rubber spatula. This folding motion should be gentle, and should be done only till the two mixtures are combined.

2 Place shrimp or crab meat atop the torn salad greens on each individual salad plate. Space the seafood evenly around the plate. Then add the avocado slices, tomato wedges, and hard-cooked egg wedges.

Crunchy Chicken Salad

½ cup Creamy Mayonnaise (see recipe, page 96)
¼ cup snipped parsley
2 tablespoons lemon juice
2 tablespoons drained capers
1 teaspoon sugar
5 cups torn romaine *or* salad greens (see pages 8–9)
12 ounces cooked chicken, cut into julienne strips (see tip box, page 15)
1 large sweet red *or* green pepper, cut into bite-size strips
½ cup sliced leeks *or* ¼ cup sliced green onion
½ cup broken walnuts

Prepare Creamy Mayonnaise (see photos 1–2, page 96). For dressing, in a small mixing bowl combine ½ cup Creamy Mayonnaise, parsley, lemon juice, drained capers, and sugar. Cover and chill.

Meanwhile, in a salad bowl combine romaine or salad greens, chicken, red or green pepper, leeks, and walnuts. Pour dressing over salad. Toss to coat. Makes 4 main-dish servings.

Mayonnaise Magic

If your mayonnaise separates, you can restore the creamy texture without wasting any of the ingredients.

Very slowly beat the separated mayonnaise mixture into an egg yolk. (You're repeating the same process you followed to make mayonnaise.) This won't work if you reverse the procedure and beat the egg yolk into the separated mayonnaise mixture.

Mix and Match Chef's Salad

This salad is so much fun to eat because you make it the way you want it. Just mix and match meats, cheeses, and veggies for a different salad every time!

⅓ cup Creamy Mayonnaise (see recipe, page 96)
3 tablespoons dairy sour cream
1 tablespoon snipped parsley
1 tablespoon snipped chives *or* sliced green onion
1 tablespoon tarragon vinegar
2 teaspoons anchovy paste
6 cups torn salad greens (see pages 8–9)
6 ounces fully cooked ham, roast beef, chicken, *or* turkey, cut into julienne strips (see tip box, page 15)
4 ounces Swiss, cheddar, American, *or* Monterey Jack cheese, cut into ¼-inch cubes
1 cup sliced fresh mushrooms *or* halved cherry tomatoes
¾ cup sliced radishes, celery, *or* cucumber
½ cup shredded carrot *or* chopped green pepper

Prepare Creamy Mayonnaise (see photos 1–2, page 96). For dressing, in a blender container or food processor bowl combine ⅓ cup Creamy Mayonnaise, sour cream, parsley, chives or green onion, tarragon vinegar, and anchovy paste. Cover and blend or process till smooth. Cover and chill.

Meanwhile, in a large salad bowl combine torn greens, meat, cheese, and vegetables. Pour dressing over salad. Toss to coat. Makes 4 main-dish servings.

B.L.T. Salad

A bacon, lettuce, and tomato sandwich, minus the bread, plus smoked turkey strips equals a great, satisfying salad!

½ cup Creamy Mayonnaise (see recipe, page 96)
1 hard-cooked egg, finely chopped
2 tablespoons finely chopped celery
1 tablespoon chili sauce
1 tablespoon finely chopped green pepper
1 tablespoon thinly sliced green onion
½ teaspoon paprika
  Dash ground red pepper
6 cups torn salad greens (see pages 8–9)
2 3-ounce packages very thinly sliced smoked turkey, cut into julienne strips (see tip box, page 15)
6 slices bacon, crisp-cooked, drained, and crumbled
2 medium tomatoes, cut into wedges
4 slices Melba toast, broken

Prepare Creamy Mayonnaise (see photos 1–2, page 96). For dressing, in a small mixing bowl combine ½ cup Creamy Mayonnaise, egg, celery, chili sauce, green pepper, green onion, paprika, and red pepper. Cover and chill.

Meanwhile, in a large salad bowl combine torn greens, turkey strips, bacon, and tomatoes. Pour dressing over salad. Toss to coat. Sprinkle Melba toast on top. Makes 4 main-dish servings.

Beef 'n' Swiss Salad

Next time you're looking for a chunky blue cheese dressing, try this one.

½ cup Creamy Mayonnaise (see recipe, page 96)
¼ cup crumbled blue cheese (1 ounce)
1 tablespoon lemon juice
1 small clove garlic, minced
¼ teaspoon Worcestershire sauce
  Dash bottled hot pepper sauce
¼ cup whipping cream
6 cups torn salad greens (see pages 8–9)
6 ounces cooked roast beef, cut into julienne strips (see tip box, page 15)
1½ cups shredded Swiss cheese (6 ounces)
  Croutons (optional)

Prepare Creamy Mayonnaise (see photos 1–2, page 96). For dressing, in a small mixing bowl combine ½ cup Creamy Mayonnaise, blue cheese, lemon juice, garlic, Worcestershire sauce, and hot pepper sauce.

In a small mixer bowl beat whipping cream with an electric mixer on high speed till soft peaks form. Gently fold whipped cream into the mayonnaise mixture (see photo 1, page 97). Cover and chill.

Meanwhile, in a large salad bowl combine torn greens, beef, and Swiss cheese. If necessary, thin dressing with a small amount of milk. Pour dressing over salad. Toss to coat. Pass croutons, if desired. Makes 6 main-dish servings.

More Salad Suppers

If you've been looking for a sensational main-dish salad, capped with a smooth, creamy dressing, look no further! Start with our basic Cooked Salad Dressing that you can jazz up. The result: a variety of delightful homemade dressings.

Need proof? Try one of the recipes in this chapter. We think you'll find the evidence simply delicious.

*Scallop Salad with
Pineapple Dressing*

Cooked Salad Dressing

2 tablespoons sugar
2 teaspoons cornstarch
1 teaspoon dry mustard
½ teaspoon salt
   Dash ground red pepper
¾ cup milk
2 slightly beaten egg yolks
¼ cup vinegar
1½ teaspoons butter *or* margarine

In a small saucepan combine sugar, cornstarch, mustard, salt, and red pepper. Stir in milk (see photo 1). Stir in egg yolks (see photo 2). Cook and stir over medium heat till bubbly, then cook and stir 2 minutes more (see photo 3). Add vinegar and butter or margarine; stir till butter is melted. Cool. Store in a tightly covered jar in refrigerator. Store up to 4 weeks in the refrigerator. If necessary, thin dressing with a small amount of milk. Makes 1 cup.

1 Add the milk all at once to the dry ingredients. Stir with a wooden spoon to thoroughly combine the milk and dry ingredients. Make sure the mixture is well-combined to avoid lumps.

2 Stir slightly beaten egg yolks into the milk mixture. The egg yolks help thicken the dressing and give it a rich, lemon-yellow color.

3 Cook and stir the dressing over medium heat till bubbly, then cook 2 minutes more. This cooks the egg yolks and cornstarch for maximum thickening power. The salad dressing will have a thick, creamy consistency and appear glossy.

Scallop Salad with Pineapple Dressing

½ cup **Cooked Salad Dressing**
    (see recipe, left)
2 **tablespoons orange marmalade**
12 **ounces fresh *or* frozen bay scallops**
2 **6-ounce packages frozen pea pods,**
    thawed
2 **11-ounce cans pineapple tidbits and**
    mandarin orange sections, chilled
    and drained
1 **cup bias-sliced celery (optional)**
    Pomegranate seeds (optional)

Prepare Cooked Salad Dressing (see photos 1–3, page 102). In a small bowl combine ½ cup Cooked Salad Dressing and orange marmalade. Cover and chill in the refrigerator.

Thaw scallops, if frozen. Add scallops to saucepan of boiling salted water. Simmer about 1 minute or till scallops are opaque and tender (see photo 1). Drain. Cover and chill.

Meanwhile, arrange pea pods on a serving platter or on 4 individual salad plates. Arrange scallops, pineapple and orange sections, and celery, if desired, beside pea pods (see photo 2). If necessary, thin dressing with a small amount of milk. Drizzle salad with dressing before serving. Garnish with pomegranate seeds, if desired. Makes 4 main-dish servings.

1 Add scallops to the boiling water. Cook about 1 minute. The scallops are done when they change from transparent to opaque.

2 Arrange scallops on top of the pea pods. Top with the pineapple tidbits and orange sections and then the celery, if desired.

Tarragon-Chicken Salad

⅔ cup Cooked Salad Dressing (see recipe, page 102)
½ teaspoon dried tarragon, crushed
4 cups torn salad greens (see pages 8–9)
8 ounces cooked chicken, cut into julienne strips (1½ cups)
½ of a 10-ounce package (1 cup) frozen peas and carrots, thawed
¾ cup shredded Swiss or Monterey Jack cheese (3 ounces)
½ cup sliced radishes

Prepare Cooked Salad Dressing (see photos 1–3, page 102). For dressing, in a small bowl combine ⅔ cup Cooked Salad Dressing and tarragon. Cover and chill.

Meanwhile, in a large salad bowl combine torn greens, chicken, peas and carrots, cheese, and radishes. Pour dressing over salad. Toss to coat. Makes 4 main-dish servings.

Herbed Ham and Asparagus Salad

½ cup Cooked Salad Dressing (see recipe, page 102)
½ teaspoon dried basil, crushed
¼ teaspoon dried savory or marjoram, crushed
¼ teaspoon dried thyme, crushed
1 10-ounce package frozen cut asparagus
4 cups torn salad greens (see pages 8–9)
1 cup cubed fully cooked ham (5 ounces)
1 cup cubed cooked chicken (5 ounces)
1 cup sliced fresh mushrooms

Prepare Cooked Salad Dressing (see photos 1–3, page 102). For dressing, in a small bowl combine ½ cup Cooked Salad Dressing, basil, savory or marjoram, and thyme. Cover and chill.

Meanwhile, cook asparagus according to package directions; drain. Cover; chill thoroughly.

In a salad bowl combine asparagus, torn greens, ham, chicken, and mushrooms. If necessary, thin dressing with a small amount of milk. Pour dressing over salad. Toss to coat. Makes 4 main-dish servings.

Robust Beef Salad

½ cup Cooked Salad Dressing (see recipe, page 102)
2 tablespoons Dijon-style mustard
Dash ground red pepper
5 cups torn salad greens (see pages 8–9)
4 ounces thinly sliced cooked beef, cut into julienne strips (see tip box, page 15)
4 ounces mozzarella cheese, cut into ¾-inch cubes
1 cup cherry tomatoes, quartered
⅔ cup thinly sliced zucchini or cucumber
2 tablespoons thinly sliced green onion

Prepare Cooked Salad Dressing (see photos 1–3, page 102). For dressing, in a small bowl combine ½ cup Cooked Salad Dressing, mustard, and ground red pepper. Cover and chill.

Meanwhile, in a salad bowl combine torn greens, beef, cheese, tomatoes, zucchini or cucumber, and green onion. Pour dressing over salad. Toss to coat. Makes 4 main-dish servings.

Curried Shrimp Salad

Curry powder often includes turmeric, cardamom, mustard, cloves, fennel, and allspice. Each curry is unique and can be made from up to 20 different spices.

½ cup Cooked Salad Dressing (see recipe, page 102)
½ cup dairy sour cream
1 teaspoon curry powder
½ cup whipping cream
1 6-ounce package curried rice mix
2 cups shelled, cooked shrimp, halved lengthwise, *or* one 16-ounce package frozen cooked shrimp, thawed and halved lengthwise
1 cup chopped celery
½ cup chopped green pepper
4 slices bacon, crisp-cooked, drained, and crumbled
   Lettuce leaves
   Shredded coconut (optional)
   Peanuts *or* cashews (optional)

Prepare Cooked Salad Dressing (see photos 1–3, page 102). For dressing, in a small mixing bowl combine ½ cup Cooked Salad Dressing, sour cream, and curry powder. In a small mixer bowl beat whipping cream with an electric mixer on high speed till soft peaks form. Gently fold whipped cream into salad dressing mixture. Cover and chill.

Meanwhile, cook rice mix according to package directions; cool. Reserve 6 shrimp for garnish; chill. In a mixing bowl combine rice, remaining shrimp, celery, green pepper, and *half* the bacon. Pour dressing over rice mixture. Toss to coat. Cover and chill.

Before serving, transfer salad to a lettuce-lined bowl. Top with the reserved shrimp and remaining bacon. Pass coconut and nuts, if desired. Makes 6 main-dish servings.

Pepperoni Salad

If pepperoni doesn't suit your taste, use sliced salami, summer sausage, or any hard, fully cooked sausage.

⅓ cup Cooked Salad Dressing (see recipe, page 102)
2 tablespoons dairy sour cream
¼ teaspoon dry mustard
⅛ teaspoon garlic powder
   Several dashes bottled hot pepper sauce
4 cups torn salad greens (see pages 8–9)
½ of a 15-ounce can garbanzo beans, drained (¾ cup)
1 3½-ounce package sliced pepperoni
2 small carrots, cut into julienne strips (see tip box, page 15)
1 large tomato, seeded and chopped (1 cup)

Prepare Cooked Salad Dressing (see photos 1–3, page 102). For dressing, in a small bowl combine ⅓ cup Cooked Salad Dressing, sour cream, mustard, garlic powder, and hot pepper sauce. Cover and chill.

Meanwhile, in a salad bowl combine torn greens, garbanzo beans, pepperoni, carrots, and tomato. Pour dressing over salad. Toss to coat. Makes 4 main-dish servings.

Salad Luncheon

When it's your turn to host the volunteer group or have the bridge club over, you'll be ready. Light and lush, this spread of salads will have your guests wanting to taste every dish—again and again!

Menu

- Caesar Salad*
- Ham Slaw Salad*
- Seafood Tabbouleh*
- Fresh Fruit Platter*
- Herb Twists*
- Lemon Bread*
- Minty Pineappleade*
- Iced Tea

*see pages 108-113

Caesar Salad

Caesar Salad

1 egg
1 clove garlic, halved
2 tablespoons olive oil *or* salad oil
2 tablespoons lemon *or* lime juice
Few dashes Worcestershire sauce
Dash bottled hot pepper sauce
5 cups torn romaine (see pages 8–9)
½ cup Garlic Croutons
¼ cup grated Parmesan cheese
Dash pepper
Rolled anchovy fillets (optional)

Allow egg to come to room temperature. To coddle egg place whole egg in a small saucepan of boiling water (see photo 1). Remove from heat; let stand 1 minute. Drain and cool slightly.

Rub a large wooden salad bowl with the cut sides of garlic clove (see photo 2). Discard garlic. Add oil, lemon or lime juice, Worcestershire sauce, and bottled hot pepper sauce. Break the coddled egg into the bowl (see photo 3). Using a fork or a wire whisk, beat till the dressing becomes creamy. Add romaine. Toss to coat (see photo 4). Sprinkle with Garlic Croutons, Parmesan cheese, and pepper; toss. If desired, top with anchovy fillets. Makes 6 servings.

Garlic Croutons: Spread both sides of four ½-inch-thick *French bread* slices with 3 tablespoons softened *butter* or *margarine*. Sprinkle with *garlic powder*. Cut bread into ¾-inch cubes (see tip box). Spread cubes on a baking sheet. Bake in a 300° oven for 12 to 15 minutes or till croutons are dry-crisp. Store in a covered container in refrigerator. Makes about 2 cups.

1 Carefully lower the egg into boiling water. Remove the pan from the heat and let stand 1 minute. During this time the egg cooks slightly, coddling it. Drain and cool the egg.

2 Using the cut sides of the garlic clove, rub the bottom and sides of the wooden salad bowl. This gives the salad just a hint of garlic without being too strong.

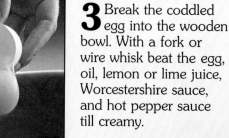

3 Break the coddled egg into the wooden bowl. With a fork or wire whisk beat the egg, oil, lemon or lime juice, Worcestershire sauce, and hot pepper sauce till creamy.

4 Add torn romaine to the salad bowl. Using 2 salad servers or a salad fork and spoon, toss the salad with a lifting motion. Toss till romaine is thoroughly coated with dressing.

Croutons: Place the French bread slices on a cutting board. Using a sharp knife, cut each slice of bread into ¾-inch-strips, then cut the strips crosswise into ¾-inch cubes.

Timetable

1 day before
- Mix the base for the Minty Pineappleade. Pour mixture into a jar. Cover and chill.
- Prepare Lemon Bread; bake. Remove bread from pan and cool on rack. Wrap and store at room temperature, so it's fresh for the luncheon.
- Prepare Seafood Tabbouleh. Cover. Place in refrigerator to chill and let flavors develop.
- Make croutons for the Caesar Salad.

2½ hrs. before
- Prepare Ham Slaw Salad. Cover and chill.
- While the salad is chilling, set out plates, flatware, napkins, glasses, and decorations. Plan a simple, buffet-style table setting. Place everything in a natural progression: plates first, food next, and the flatware and glasses last. Help guests by setting out flatware wrapped in napkins.

50 mins. before
- Tear romaine for Caesar Salad.
- Prepare assorted fruits for Fresh Fruit Platter; brush with lemon juice, if desired. Make the dressing.
- Prepare Herb Twists and top with desired coatings. Bake. Meanwhile, coddle egg for the Caesar Salad.

15 mins. before
- Turn salads into serving bowls and garnish.
- Cut Lemon Bread into slices.
- Make dressing for the Caesar Salad and toss salad ingredients

At Serving Time
- Place ice cubes in glasses. Add carbonated water to the Minty Pineappleade base; stir.
- Now, relax and enjoy your guests.

Ham Slaw Salad

3 cups coarsely shredded green cabbage
(see photo 1, page 14)
2 cups diced fully cooked ham *or* corned
beef (12 ounces)
¾ cup chopped green pepper
½ cup shredded carrot (see photo 4,
page 15)
⅓ cup dairy sour cream
⅓ cup bottled creamy cucumber salad
dressing
Cabbage leaves (optional)

In a bowl combine shredded cabbage, ham or corned beef, green pepper, and carrot. For dressing, combine sour cream and cucumber dressing. Pour dressing over cabbage mixture; toss to coat. Cover; chill 2 to 24 hours.

Before serving, spoon salad into a cabbage-lined bowl or hollowed-out cabbage, if desired. Makes 6 main-dish servings.

Herb Twists

No eggs on hand? Brush the biscuit ropes with milk, and then sprinkle on cheese, poppy seed, or sesame seed. (Pictured on page 106.)

2 packages (20) refrigerated biscuits
1 beaten egg
1 tablespoon water
Grated Parmesan cheese, poppy seed,
or sesame seed, toasted

With hands, roll each biscuit into an 8-inch rope. Moisten hands, if necessary (ropes will shrink to 6 inches). Twist 2 ropes together.

In a small bowl stir together egg and water. Brush tops of twists with egg-water mixture. Sprinkle with cheese, poppy seed, or sesame seed. Place twists on a greased baking sheet. Bake in a 375° oven for 15 to 18 minutes or till golden brown. Makes 10 twists.

Fresh Fruit Platter

If you're looking to cut calories, enjoy this fruit platter with little or no dressing.

3 tablespoons sugar
2 tablespoons orange juice *or*
unsweetened pineapple juice
½ teaspoon dry mustard
¼ teaspoon poppy seed (optional)
½ cup salad oil
4 cups assorted fruit*

In a small mixer bowl combine sugar, orange juice or pineapple juice, dry mustard, and poppy seed, if desired. Add salad oil, a small amount at a time, beating with a rotary beater after each addition.

Arrange fruit on a serving platter in a decorative fashion. Pass the dressing; drizzle over fruit. Makes 6 servings.

*Choose from the following fruit: halved strawberries; blueberries; raspberries; sliced kiwi fruit; melon slices, balls, *or* cubes; peach *or* nectarine slices; pineapple chunks; orange sections; *or* sliced papaya *or* mango.

Lemon Bread

1¾ **cups all-purpose flour**
2 **teaspoons baking powder**
2 **teaspoons finely shredded lemon peel**
½ **teaspoon salt**
1 **beaten egg**
¾ **cup milk**
¾ **cup sugar**
¼ **cup cooking oil**
1 **tablespoon lemon juice**

Grease an 8x4x2-inch loaf pan; set aside. In a medium mixing bowl stir together flour, baking powder, lemon peel, and salt.

Combine egg, milk, sugar, oil, and lemon juice. Add to flour mixture, stirring just till moistened. Turn batter into prepared pan. Bake in a 350° oven for 50 to 55 minutes. Cool in pan 10 minutes. Remove from pan. Cool on wire rack. Wrap in foil or clear plastic wrap; store overnight. Makes 1 loaf.

Minty Pineappleade

2 **small pineapples *or* one 20-ounce can crushed pineapple (juice pack)***
1 **cup sugar**
¼ **cup lightly packed fresh mint leaves *or* 1 tablespoon dried mint**
3 **tablespoons lime juice**
1 **16-ounce bottle carbonated water Ice cubes**

Remove crown from pineapple. Cut off the peel. Halve pineapple lengthwise; cut out core. Finely chop pineapple (should measure about 3 cups). Place chopped pineapple or *undrained* canned pineapple in a 2-quart saucepan. Add sugar and 1 cup *water*. Bring to boiling; reduce heat. Cover and simmer for 15 minutes.

◄ *Pictured opposite: Seafood Tabbouleh, Minty Pineappleade, and Lemon Bread*

Meanwhile, tie fresh or dried mint in a piece of cheesecloth. Place mint bag in pineapple mixture. Let stand, covered, about 1½ hours or till slightly cool. Strain; discard mint. Reserve the pineapple for another use. Stir lime juice into pineapple liquid. Pour into jars or an airtight container. Cover and chill.

Before serving, slowly add carbonated water. Serve over ice cubes. Garnish with pineapple wedges and fresh mint leaves, if desired. Makes about 4 cups.

*****Note:** If you're using canned pineapple, reduce the amount of water to ¾ cup.

Seafood Tabbouleh

¾ **cup bulgur wheat**
2 **6-ounce packages frozen crab meat and shrimp, thawed**
1 **medium cucumber, seeded and finely chopped**
½ **cup snipped parsley**
¼ **cup thinly sliced green onion**
¼ **cup salad oil**
¼ **cup lemon juice**
1 **tablespoon snipped fresh mint *or* 1 teaspoon dried mint, crushed**
¼ **teaspoon salt**
⅛ **teaspoon pepper**
1 **medium tomato, seeded and chopped Tomato rose (optional) Mint leaves (optional)**

Place bulgur in a colander. Rinse with cold water. Drain well. In a large bowl combine drained bulgur, crab meat and shrimp, cucumber, parsley, and onion. For dressing, in a screw-top jar combine oil, lemon juice, snipped mint, salt, and pepper. Cover and shake well. Pour over bulgur mixture. Toss to coat. Cover and chill overnight.

Before serving, stir in chopped tomato. Garnish with a tomato rose and mint leaves, if desired. Makes 6 main-dish servings.

Red-tip leaf lettuce

Romaine

Boston lettuce

Greens Galore

A salad overflowing with fresh greens is the perfect way to enjoy garden-fresh flavor year-round. Although iceberg remains a popular choice among salad lovers, it's fun to be daring and explore what other greens have to offer. Add pizzazz to your next salad by using a combination of greens that differ in flavor, texture, and color. We've simplified things for you a bit. Here's information on how to identify and select your greens.

Green beginnings

Choosing greens is the first step in making any salad memorable. Select the freshest greens possible, avoiding limp or bruised greens. Don't wash until needed. Then, when ready to use, wash, drain, and pat greens dry. Place leftovers in a plastic bag or covered container to keep them crisp. Store in the refrigerator.

To serve, tear leaves to expose the insides and allow the greens to absorb the dressing. Cutting them bruises and discolors the leaves.

Romaine

Romaine or cos lettuce originated on the Greek island of Cos. Romaine lettuce has elongated, coarse leaves with a heavy rib running down the middle of each leaf. Leaves near the outside of the head are long and large; the center leaves are more tender and delicate. Romaine is crisp, with a refreshingly pungent flavor.

Leaf lettuce

Iceberg lettuce

Bibb lettuce

Boston

Boston lettuce, also known as butterhead or butter, is often confused with Bibb lettuce. Boston is a medium, round-headed lettuce with soft, waxy leaves. In keeping with its delicate appearance, Boston lettuce has a delicate, mild flavor.

Bibb

Bibb lettuce, sometimes called limestone, is shaped similar to Boston lettuce and is a member of the butterhead family. Bibb lettuce is somewhat smaller than Boston lettuce. The small, cup-shaped leaves have a soft, delicate texture and lend a subtly sweet flavor to salads. These small, tender leaves also make attractive serving containers and plate liners for individual servings of salad.

Iceberg

The most popular salad green is iceberg lettuce, also called crisphead or head lettuce. When shopping for this salad favorite, look for a solid, compact head with tight leaves. The leaves will vary from pale green in the center to medium green on the outside. Iceberg, one of the crispest lettuces, has a mild, watery flavor, so it nicely complements salads containing stronger greens.

Leaf

There are several types of leaf lettuce. The flavor is similar in all of them, but the leaves may be green to bronze to red-tipped. When selecting any type of leaf lettuce, look for large, leafy bunches of lettuce with tender leaves. The sweet yet delicate flavor blends well in any salad.

Escarole

Chicory

More Glorious Greens

If you're unfamiliar with names like escarole, sorrel, or watercress, you're not alone. Because these greens are not as readily available and well-known as others, you might not know how delicious they are. Browse through this section and then sample some of these special greens in your next salad.

Escarole

Coming from the endive family, escarole is often known as broad-leafed endive. Escarole has broader, less curly leaves than chicory. Escarole's color can range from dark green to pale yellow.

When purchasing escarole, choose leaves that are fresh and tender. This coarse-textured green will add a slightly bitter flavor to your salads.

Chicory

Another member of the endive family, chicory is also known as curly endive. This prickly textured green adds zest to salads, with its somewhat sharp flavor. In addition to adding pep, this green is loaded with vitamin A.

Look for chicory with narrow, curly leaves. Chicory combines well with milder greens.

Spinach

Sorrel

Watercress

Rocket

Spinach

Spinach has often been reputed to be the vegetable that builds muscles and strength. It's true that this vegetable is full of vitamins and iron—and it's also delicious both cooked and raw.

When used raw, as a salad green, the dark green leaves add color and character to a salad. Available year-round, spinach should have dark green leaves that are crisp and free of moisture or mold.

Watercress

As the name suggests, watercress grows in freshwater ponds and streams. This pungently flavored green is a lively addition to any salad. Look for large, dark green leaves. As a rule, the darker and larger the leaves, the better the watercress.

Watercress can also serve as an attractive, edible garnish.

Sorrel

Sorrel, also known as sourgrass, looks almost like spinach, but the leaves are somewhat smaller. Sorrel, however, is not as common as spinach and may require some extra shopping effort.

Look for young, tender sorrel leaves that are free from blemishes. Sorrel's lemony flavor gives a sharp, slightly acidic taste to salads.

Rocket

Rocket, also known as arugula, is Italian in origin. While this green is often hard to find, taking the extra time to search for it is worth it. Its dark green leaves lend a peppery flavor to any salad. Choose young, tender leaves for the best flavor.

Hazelnut oil   *Olive oil*   *Almond oil*

Oil Options

No matter what you're preparing—a creamy mayonnaise dressing or a sophisticated vinaigrette—it's always important to select an oil that will enhance each salad individually. By learning to identify different types of oils, you can choose an oil that complements your salad.

Nut-Flavored Oil

1½ **cups unblanched shelled whole hazelnuts, almonds, *or* walnuts (about 7½ ounces)**
2½ **cups salad oil**

Place nuts in a blender container or food processor bowl. Cover and blend or process till chopped. Through the opening in the lid, and with the blender on slow speed, gradually add *½ cup* of oil. Blend till nuts are finely chopped.

Transfer nut mixture to a saucepan. Place a candy thermometer in the pan. Cook over low heat, stirring occasionally, till thermometer registers 160°. Remove from heat; cool slightly. Combine nut mixture with remaining oil. Cover tightly; let stand in a cool place for 1 to 2 weeks.

Line a colander with fine-woven cloth or cup-shaped coffee filter. Pour oil mixture through colander; let drain in a bowl. Discard nut paste. Pour strained oil into a 1½-pint jar; cover tightly. Refrigerate up to 3 months. Makes 2½ cups.

Walnut oil   *Peanut oil*   *Sesame oil*

Vegetable Oils

Because of their subtle flavors these all-purpose oils are used in the kitchen for baking and frying. They also work well in salads where other flavors dominate. The most common vegetable oils are corn, safflower, sunflower, cottonseed, coconut, and soybean.

Hazelnut Oil

Hazelnut oil, also called filbert oil, is a golden-color oil. Like walnut oil, it has a unique, nutty flavor.

Olive Oil

The color of olive oil ranges from golden to a greenish hue. Spanish and Greek olive oils tend to be stronger than Italian or French oils. Olive oil flavors range from fruity and mellow to sharply distinct.

The finest olive oil is labeled "extra virgin." This oil has less than one percent of oleic acid. "Virgin" has slightly lower standards with a higher oleic acid content. Because these oils have not been heat-treated or preserved, they should be kept for only a month or two.

Almond Oil

Almond oil is a clear, pale oil. Its delicate flavor adds interest to salad dressings.

Walnut Oil

This is a rich, golden-colored oil. It contributes a nutty flavor to some dressings, but is too harsh for strong-flavored dressings. It is not recommended for frying or baking.

Peanut Oil

Peanut oil is also referred to as groundnut oil. It blends well in salad dressings because of its delicate flavor. Or, use it for frying—it's odorless.

Sesame Oil

There are two types of sesame oil. One, a thick, brown oil, is made from toasted sesame seed. It has a concentrated flavor and is used in very small amounts to flavor dressings.

The other type of sesame seed oil is pale yellow and is made from untoasted sesame seed. Its bland flavor is good for salads with stronger flavors.

Mint
vinegar

Tarragon
vinegar

Garlic
vinegar

Flavored Vinegars

Flavored vinegars are making a comeback. Why? Because they add character to salads, sauces, marinades, soups, and stews. These vinegars are a delicious way to add pizzazz to your favorite dishes. Look for your favorite flavored vinegar in the store, or try making your own.

Raspberry Vinegar

2 cups fresh raspberries *or* two 10-ounce
    packages frozen raspberries, thawed
    and drained
4 cups cider vinegar
2 cups dry red wine

Rinse fresh raspberries with cold water and drain well. In a large bowl combine raspberries, cider vinegar, and wine. Cover and let stand overnight. In a stainless steel or enamel saucepan heat vinegar mixture to boiling; boil, uncovered, for 3 minutes. Cool.

Strain mixture, discarding solids. Pour into bottles; cover tightly. Let the vinegar age for 2 to 4 weeks before using. Store in cool, dark place. Makes 6 cups.

Raspberry vinegar

Basil vinegar

Lemon vinegar

Vinegar beginnings

Distilled, cider, and wine vinegar are the three most-common vinegars. Distilled or white vinegar is a colorless vinegar made from grain mash. The distilling process removes any flavor and leaves only an acidic taste. Cider vinegar, made from apples, is a golden-brown vinegar with a slightly fruity flavor. In wine vinegars the color and flavor of the vinegar depends on the type of wine used. White wine produces a lighter-tasting vinegar than red wine.

Vinegar variety

To make flavored vinegars, start with a base of cider, distilled, or wine vinegar. Your choice of a base depends on how you plan to flavor your vinegar. Wine vinegars are good with herbs and spices. Fruits and edible flowers go well with distilled vinegar. Try using cider vinegar with spices.

How to flavor vinegars

Flavored vinegars can be prepared in two ways. The quickest method is heating the vinegar in a stainless steel or enamel pan until hot, but not boiling. Pour the vinegar over the herbs, seed, fruit, or spice. Cover with cheesecloth and let stand in a warm, dark place for one to two weeks. Then, filter the vinegar through several layers of cheesecloth and pour it into bottles.

Or, pour the vinegar directly over the ingredients and let it stand for a month.

When sampling vinegar, trust your taste buds. If the vinegar is too strong, add some plain vinegar. If it's too weak, add some seasoning. Once you've tried a variety of vinegars, try combining flavors. Mix two or three ingredients, like raspberry and mint, lemon and garlic, or peaches and cloves.

Nutrition Analysis Chart

Use these analyses to compare nutritional values of different recipes. This information was calculated using Agriculture Handbook Number 456, published by the United States Department of Agriculture, as the primary source.

In compiling the nutrition analyses, we made the following assumptions:
● For all of the main-dish meat recipes, the nutrition analyses were calculated using weights and measures for cooked meat.

● Garnishes and optional ingredients were not included in the nutrition analyses.
● If a marinade was brushed over a food during cooking, the analysis includes all of the marinade.
● When two ingredient options appear in a recipe, calculations were made using the first one.
● For ingredients of variable weight (such as "2½- to 3-pound broiler-fryer chicken") or for recipes with a serving range ("Makes 4 to 6 servings"), calculations were made using the first figure.

	Per Serving						Percent USRDA Per Serving								
	Calories	Protein (g)	Carbohydrate (g)	Fat (g)	Sodium (mg)	Potassium (mg)	Protein	Vitamin A	Vitamin C	Thiamine	Riboflavin	Niacin	Calcium	Iron
Main-Dish Salads														
Avocado and Egg Salad (p. 29)	501	17	8	46	555	689	25	31	26	14	27	8	8	18
Beef 'n' Swiss Salad (p. 99)	399	18	4	35	352	335	27	66	35	5	17	8	33	14
B.L.T. Salad (p. 99)	426	21	12	33	413	576	33	34	41	14	16	25	7	18
Broccoli-Salmon Salad (p. 26)	384	27	6	28	229	756	41	29	67	6	18	44	25	10
Cheesy Shrimp Salad (p. 28)	427	25	7	34	462	374	39	25	47	6	22	5	54	12
Chicken and Curry Salad (p. 47)	544	25	22	41	364	669	38	19	17	9	12	40	7	16
Chicken Salad in Tortilla Bowls (p. 92)	389	27	25	21	215	599	42	30	78	9	24	41	12	18
Confetti Tuna Salad (p. 28)	193	18	7	10	540	481	28	65	12	9	9	35	6	10
Creamy Chicken-and-Rice Salad (p. 69)	333	21	27	15	503	531	32	24	28	17	14	31	10	14
Crunchy Chicken Salad (p. 98)	486	30	11	37	447	743	47	72	182	13	17	41	10	19
Curried Shrimp Salad (p. 105)	339	20	29	15	398	408	31	14	33	14	10	19	13	14
Fruited Chicken Salad (p. 29)	517	26	32	34	311	834	40	20	28	13	16	37	5	16
Ham and Lima Salad (p. 68)	613	20	41	41	954	421	30	17	57	29	14	19	6	21
Ham-Pineapple Salad (p. 28)	260	16	13	16	542	358	25	4	31	28	13	14	6	12
Ham Slaw Salad (p. 111)	235	11	6	19	445	281	17	25	69	18	8	10	4	9
Herbed Ham and Asparagus Salad (p. 104)	243	23	10	13	454	631	35	29	41	24	24	30	8	19
Layered Reuben Salad (p. 44)	617	26	19	50	1147	342	40	23	41	9	24	11	33	22
Mix and Match Chef's Salad (p. 98)	414	20	8	34	642	559	31	49	27	21	23	15	32	15
Pepperoni Salad (p. 105)	236	10	16	15	622	430	15	50	21	12	10	9	8	13
Robust Beef Salad (p. 104)	246	20	11	14	478	436	30	33	32	7	19	10	35	17
Salmon Salad in Bread Bowls (p. 93)	566	37	57	22	1170	835	57	14	15	25	23	62	35	30
Scallop Salad with Pineapple Dressing (p. 103)	228	23	26	5	393	493	36	17	33	12	10	7	14	20
Seafood Salad (p. 97)	423	23	13	32	341	920	36	41	53	13	19	22	13	21

	Per Serving						Percent USRDA Per Serving							
	Calories	Protein (g)	Carbohydrate (g)	Fat (g)	Sodium (mg)	Potassium (mg)	Protein	Vitamin A	Vitamin C	Thiamine	Riboflavin	Niacin	Calcium	Iron
Main-Dish Salads *(continued)*														
Seafood Tabbouleh (p. 113)	223	12	24	10	93	203	6	13	35	7	4	8	3	9
Shrimp and Spaetzle Salad (p. 63)	319	20	23	17	365	380	31	57	48	12	12	13	13	22
Tarragon-Chicken Salad (p. 104)	275	27	13	13	443	538	41	67	25	11	19	28	29	15
Side-Dish Salads														
All-American Layered Salad (p. 42)	556	11	11	53	609	355	17	88	28	15	14	7	22	13
Apple-Orange Salad (p. 47)	204	5	20	13	64	396	8	33	43	18	9	5	7	11
Apple-Raisin Salad (p. 80)	150	3	37	0	72	240	4	3	5	2	2	1	2	6
Asparagus and Pasta Salad (p. 60)	199	6	22	10	174	326	10	21	46	9	7	7	7	9
Avocado Fruit Freeze (p. 32)	248	3	30	14	45	332	4	11	18	6	9	4	4	3
Beet-Spinach Salad (p. 10)	179	5	11	14	647	509	8	136	75	6	13	3	11	17
Berry-Stuffed Papayas (p. 90)	188	3	35	6	14	601	4	55	171	11	8	5	7	7
Blue Cheese Garden Salad (p. 55)	259	7	12	22	337	530	11	182	184	11	21	7	17	10
Broccoli-Mushroom Salad (p. 17)	96	3	7	7	102	315	5	23	93	6	14	8	5	6
Burgundy-Grape Mold (p. 80)	266	4	44	8	59	151	6	8	79	5	6	2	4	5
Caesar Salad (p. 108)	109	4	6	8	98	153	6	21	18	4	6	2	9	6
Caraway Cabbage Salad (p. 38)	106	1	6	9	104	195	2	8	76	3	2	1	3	3
Cavatelli-Artichoke Salad (p. 61)	532	16	80	18	219	569	25	19	35	63	37	37	8	22
Chutney Salad (p. 10)	119	4	17	5	34	325	6	21	17	5	6	9	7	8
Confetti Salad in Pepper Shells (p. 92)	127	9	8	7	214	293	14	31	179	6	13	3	7	5
Cranberry-Nog Mold (p. 83)	242	5	46	5	72	152	7	5	12	2	8	1	9	2
Cranberry-Orange Salad (p. 74)	189	2	45	1	46	69	3	1	30	1	1	0	1	2
Cranberry-Pear Salad (p. 22)	123	1	31	1	3	202	2	2	35	4	3	1	2	3
Creamy Macaroni-Fruit Salad (p. 61)	192	3	24	10	18	185	5	9	14	10	6	3	3	5
Creamy Potato Salad (p. 52)	367	5	24	29	706	532	7	6	32	8	6	8	3	7
Crouton Salad Bowl (p. 10)	181	6	8	15	302	259	9	20	12	4	7	2	17	11
Crunchy Coleslaw with Creamy Dressing (p. 16)	88	1	5	7	155	172	2	24	71	3	4	2	4	3
Crunchy Coleslaw with Vinaigrette Dressing (p. 16)	63	1	5	5	58	170	2	23	71	3	4	2	3	2
Curried Fruit Salad (p. 44)	292	5	63	5	58	744	7	17	39	14	13	6	10	11
Date Waldorf Salad (p. 22)	279	3	29	19	99	344	4	6	36	7	4	3	5	7
Dilled Vegetable Combo (p. 39)	115	2	7	10	108	223	3	63	43	5	4	3	3	5
Dilled Vegetable Vinaigrette (p. 52)	112	3	11	7	41	571	4	94	35	8	17	15	3	8
Easy Apricot Salad (p. 23)	186	3	28	8	28	384	5	26	25	8	9	4	7	6
Fiesta Salad (p. 45)	213	9	15	14	478	231	13	9	11	3	7	3	17	7
French-Onion Fling (p. 10)	230	3	13	19	393	244	4	4	6	3	7	5	1	3
Fresh Fruit Platter (p. 111)	230	1	17	18	1	176	1	5	64	5	3	2	2	4
Frosty Tropical Salads (p. 33)	223	4	14	18	79	230	6	16	11	5	7	2	4	4
Fruit and Rice Salad (p. 69)	208	4	26	10	163	200	7	7	8	9	4	11	4	6
Fruit-Filled Nectarines (p. 92)	143	1	38	0	19	511	2	51	46	3	6	8	2	6
Fruity Pasta Salad (p. 63)	125	4	26	1	25	212	5	13	34	11	7	7	2	6
Ginger Fruit Bowl (p. 20)	190	3	32	7	55	545	4	15	219	8	12	8	9	14
Golden Salad (p. 75)	189	3	47	0	72	248	4	4	17	5	2	1	2	4
Grape and Pineapple Salad (p. 47)	97	2	15	4	14	189	2	6	11	4	4	2	4	3
Greek Layered Salad (p. 45)	87	5	6	5	317	257	8	43	30	5	8	3	14	9
Greek-Style Salad (p. 11)	108	3	7	9	168	166	4	46	27	3	4	1	7	7

	Per Serving					Percent USRDA Per Serving							
	Calories	Protein (g)	Carbohydrate (g)	Fat (g)	Sodium (mg)	Potassium (mg)	Protein	Vitamin A	Vitamin C	Thiamine	Riboflavin	Niacin	Calcium	Iron

Side-Dish Salads *(continued)*

	Calories	Protein (g)	Carbohydrate (g)	Fat (g)	Sodium (mg)	Potassium (mg)	Protein	Vitamin A	Vitamin C	Thiamine	Riboflavin	Niacin	Calcium	Iron
Italian Bean and Potato Salad (p. 50)	259	6	26	15	488	658	10	10	39	13	13	15	7	8
Layered Vegetable Aspic (p. 78)	80	7	11	2	521	134	10	24	29	6	3	10	2	4
Lime and Grape Salad (p. 74)	107	2	26	0	47	177	3	1	4	2	1	1	1	2
Marinated Mushrooms (p. 38)	94	2	6	7	193	354	4	4	39	6	17	14	2	5
Mushroom-and-Bacon Rice Salad (p. 68)	148	3	14	9	167	189	5	5	15	8	9	9	1	5
Mushroom-Avocado Stuffed Tomatoes (p. 93)	260	3	11	24	180	775	5	27	64	11	15	13	3	7
Oriental Rice Salad (p. 66)	158	4	20	8	198	75	6	3	8	7	7	6	2	7
Oriental Toss (p. 11)	98	1	7	8	155	131	2	11	13	2	3	1	2	5
Parsnip Salad (p. 17)	141	2	14	9	338	403	3	3	61	4	5	1	5	4
Perky Potato Salad (p. 53)	189	2	16	14	138	394	3	8	49	6	3	7	2	4
Plum-Banana Salad (p. 23)	168	1	39	3	6	388	2	15	27	3	4	5	2	4
Potato and Beet Salad (p. 55)	202	3	26	11	276	517	4	4	35	7	4	7	3	7
Rum Fruit Molds (p. 81)	133	2	21	4	47	155	3	9	2	3	1	2	1	3
Shells and Cheeses Salad (p. 60)	400	16	26	26	398	247	25	17	19	19	21	10	29	9
Snappy Tomato Cubes (p. 75)	136	4	25	3	242	305	6	16	39	4	4	4	4	5
Spiced Fruit Salad (p. 39)	111	1	28	1	3	313	2	15	90	4	6	5	2	6
Strawberry and Apple Salad (p. 72)	141	2	35	0	70	176	3	1	5	1	1	0	1	4
Summertime Melon-Lime Mold (p. 83)	146	2	36	0	9	161	3	1	24	2	1	2	1	2
Sweet 'n' Sour Salad (p. 16)	109	2	14	6	13	208	3	44	19	8	3	3	3	6
Sweet Potato and Pecan Salad (p. 52)	321	5	35	19	352	490	8	194	59	17	9	5	8	8
Tater Salad (p. 53)	180	4	36	3	539	368	7	20	76	7	6	6	3	7
Three-Bean Carrot Salad (p. 36)	255	4	21	19	279	349	6	125	68	6	6	4	7	14
Three-Fruit Salad (p. 22)	127	1	33	0	3	280	2	19	79	3	5	5	2	6
Tomato-Parmesan Toss (p. 8)	139	4	7	11	360	234	5	20	23	5	6	3	8	6
Tortellini and Cucumber Salad (p. 58)	323	10	24	21	456	251	15	8	16	22	10	10	17	11
Vegetable Potpourri (p. 14)	127	3	9	10	129	339	4	27	76	5	6	4	6	4
Very Berry Puff (p. 74)	91	3	20	0	67	103	5	0	0	1	4	0	6	0
Wilted Chinese Cabbage Salad (p. 87)	138	5	12	8	549	511	7	59	79	12	10	7	7	13
Wilted Romaine Salad (p. 86)	107	2	8	8	83	236	3	24	54	7	4	3	5	6
Zippy Gazpacho Molds (p. 81)	26	3	4	0	185	246	4	13	30	4	2	4	2	3
Miscellaneous														
Cooked Salad Dressing (p. 102)	25	1	3	1	78	19	1	2	0	1	2	0	2	1
Creamy Mayonnaise (p. 96)	101	0	0	11	56	5	1	1	1	0	0	0	0	0
Herb Twists (p. 111)	198	5	30	6	569	74	8	2	0	12	11	8	6	8
Lemon Bread (p. 113)	129	2	21	4	113	36	3	1	1	6	5	4	4	3
Minty Pineappleade (p. 113)	164	0	43	0	1	103	0	1	22	4	1	1	1	2
Nut-Flavored Oil (p. 118)	142	1	1	15	0	46	2	0	0	1	3	1	1	2
Raspberry Vinegar (p. 120)	7	0	1	0	0	19	0	0	1	0	0	0	0	1

Index

Index

Have BETTER HOMES AND
GARDENS® magazine delivered
to your door. For information,
write to: MR. ROBERT AUSTIN
P.O. BOX 4536
DES MOINES, IA 50336